DEDICATION

To the Almighty,
for His boundless grace, strength, and guidance through every step of this journey.

To my parents,
whose unconditional love and values are the foundation of all that I am.

To my sister,
for her silent strength, unwavering support, and constant encouragement.

To my husband,
for his patience, belief, and being my greatest cheerleader.

To my teachers,
who shaped my thoughts and ignited my passion for learning.

And to my friends,
for their companionship, motivation, and presence through thick and thin.

FOREWORD

It gives me immense pleasure to present this book, which is a sincere and scholarly effort to contribute meaningfully to the academic and clinical understanding of the subject. We have combined deep theoretical knowledge with practical insights, making this work both informative and thought-provoking. The book reflects a commitment to research, clarity in presentation, and a genuine passion for the discipline. I am confident that this work will serve as a valuable resource for students, academicians, and professionals alike, inspiring further exploration and dialogue in the field

PREFACE

This book is a culmination of my library dissertation titled "Glycosylation Process of Oral Squamous Cell Carcinomas: Functions in Stemness, Tumorigenesis, and Metastasis." The subject of glycosylation, though complex and highly specialized, holds immense significance in understanding the molecular mechanisms driving cancer progression, particularly in oral squamous cell carcinomas (OSCC). Through this work, I have attempted to delve into the intricate roles of aberrant glycosylation in cancer cell behavior—its contribution to stemness, invasion, and metastasis—and to explore its potential implications in diagnosis and targeted therapy.

The motivation behind this compilation stems from a strong academic interest in tumor biology and molecular oncology. I have endeavored to present the current state of knowledge in a structured, comprehensive, and accessible manner, hoping it will serve as a valuable reference for students, clinicians, and researchers alike.

I sincerely thank my mentors, teachers, and peers for their guidance, support, and insightful discussions throughout this journey. I also extend my gratitude to all those who made indirect yet valuable contributions through encouragement and feedback. I hope that this book sparks further inquiry and interest in the unexplored dimensions of glycosylation in cancer biology.

ACKNOWLEDGEMENT

*No endeavor can start, continue and complete without the blessing of **Almighty God** and the guidance of revered and beloved teachers of this esteemed institution. Their constant pursuit of excellence has enabled me to complete the present project successfully.*

*I begin by expressing my affectionate thanks to my parents (**Mr. John Thomas & Mrs. Jolly John**), my beloved grandmothers **Mrs. Annamma Thomas & Mrs. Thankamma John**, my younger sisters **Sharin John, Tania Thomas, Tenzie Thomas**, my husband **Dr. Raj Yash**, and other family members whose unforgettable sacrifices and blessings provided me the opportunity to be educated and without their encouragement, support and love I would never have been able to complete this study.*

*It is my proud privilege to acknowledge with a deep sense of gratitude and devotion the keen personal interest and invaluable guidance rendered to me by an esteemed and revered teacher, guide, and illuminating supervisor **Dr. Shalini Gupta** (Professor), Department of Oral & Maxillofacial Pathology & Oral Microbiology, King George Medical University, Lucknow, for her untiring efforts, advice, and masterly guidance. Her constant support and active interest had brought this work of mine to its present form. It is a great honor for me to have worked under her.*

*I pay my sincere tribute to **Dr. Shaleen Chandra** (Professor & Head), Department of Oral& Maxillofacial Pathology and Oral Microbiology, King George Medical University, Lucknow, for his kind cooperation, constructive criticism, and valuable suggestions provided to me during this study.*

*It is with a feeling of loving fondness that I recall the names of my seniors **Dr. Tanveer Fatima, Dr. Manjeet Kour Mehta, Dr. Nikhil Gupta,** and my colleagues **Dr. Kriti, Dr. Eram, Dr. Ramya** and my loving juniors **Dr. Ayushi, Dr. Priya, Dr. Roshna Dr. Saloni, Dr. Arushi, Dr. Lakshimi, and Dr. Riya**. I am extremely thankful to my dear friends **Dr. Alisha, Dr. Priyam, Dr. Jyoti,** and **Dr. Bandhavi** who stood by me and supported me at every stage of work*

Dr. Sharon John

Glycosylation process of Oral squamous cell carcinomas: Functions in stemness, tumorgenesis and metastasis

CONTENTS

17. Enzymes involved in O-N glycosylation and metastasis

18. Target proteins of N-glycosylation involved in metastasis

19. Glycosaminoglycans (GAGs)

20. Proteoglycans involved in metastasis

21. GAG-related enzymes involved in metastasis

22. Prognosticators of OSCC

23. Bibliography

1. INTRODUCTION

One of the most essential components of a cell is glycans. This tiny molecular component is often overlooked, but to underestimate its role in physiological processes would be unwise. Glycans and the process by which they are altered and formed, known as glycosylation, are responsible for signal transduction, cell differentiation, cell adhesion, motility, host pathogen interactions, tumor cell formation, and the development of metastatic disease [1]. As a result, the subject has garnered significant attention and shown glycosylation is inextricably involved with tumor immunogenicity. The alteration of glycans has also been implicated in cancer progression[1]. Thus, it comes to no surprise that to further our understanding of glycosylation and its role in tumor immune evasion and cancer proliferation, we must dive further into how alterations in O-linked and N-linked glycosylation lead to cancer virulence and whether understanding the mechanism behind these changes can lead to translational therapeutic strategies. This chapter hopes to elucidate the existing literature on the role of glycosylation in antitumor immunity and set the stage for potential therapeutic strategies that those working in the fields of oncology, immuno-oncology, and radiobiology can put forth.

Glycans are vital in the cell biology of many cancers. They are responsible for tumor cell dissociation, metastasis formation, cell matrix interaction, angiogenesis, immune escape, cell signaling and communication, among other things[2]. Tumor cells often display glycosylation alterations especially in cancer types such as lung cancer and glioblastoma (GB)[3] in fact, it is the over expression of certain proteoglycans that characterize certain cancers[7]. Alteration of the serglycin proteoglycan has been linked to promoting progression and metastasis in triple-negative breast cancer, and heparan sulfate proteoglycan alterations have been implicated in colorectal cancer[8].

Proteoglycans can control the activation of such tyrosine receptors such as MET (hepatocyte growth factor receptor), EGFR (epidermal growth factor receptor), and IGF-1R (insulin growth factor receptor). In fact N-glycans are often covalently linked to asparagine (asn) and receptors that are involved in oncogenesis, for instance, IGFR and EGFR tend to have more N-glycan sites[2]. Ogata et al. corroborate this in a study which found that malignant cells had more N-linked sugar chains than normal cells. The relationship of cancer to N-linked glycosylation has sparked much research into inhibiting that pathway in the hopes of curtailing cancer progression. Further studies into the implications of N-linked glycosylation in cancer show that increase branching of B1-6 is correlated with metastasis. Moreover, the B1, 6-N-acetylglucosaminyl transferase V (GnT-V) is responsible for cancer cell invasion and migration[9]. N-linked glycosylation is by no means the only form of glycosylation that is tied to cancer. Abnormal expression of the O-glycosyltransferase enzymes is associated with multiple cancers, including lung and pancreatic types[10]. Park et al. in 2010, showed that enzymes associated with the O-linked pathway can lead to the development and progression of breast cancer[11]. They also found that the expression of GALNT6 an enzyme associated with O-linked glycosylation has been shown to glycosylate the mucin 1 (MUC1) oncoprotein, which contributes to carcinogenesis by interfering with B-catenin and E-cadherin. The group postulates that enzymes such as GALNT14 and GALNT6 could serve as predictive biomarkers in the fight against cancer[11]. The expression of truncated O-glycan structures has been linked to tumor cell epitopes and metastatic ability in cancers ranging from the colon, stomach, pancreas, and lung[12]. O-linked and N-linked oligosaccharides are major components of mucins and multiple mucin domains regulate components of the tumor microenvironment, which tie into glycosylation's role in tumor immunity. Last, but certainly not least, altered lectins and their relationship to glycans also have been shown to induce cancer development and proliferation. Tumor-associated glycans are dependent on lectin binding [9]. For example, galectins, such as galectin-1 (Gal-1) induce T-cell apoptosis causing angiogenesis and immunosuppression in several cancers such as melanoma, neuroblastoma, and lung cancers. Furthermore, selectin ligands are associated with mucins such as MUC1, MUC2 and MUC4 and interactions with these selectins 4 can lead to metastases development[15,16]. Whether it be alterations in N-linked glycans, O-linked glycans, or lectins, there is an undeniable association between aberrant glycan structures and cancer. Aberrant glycome of tumors might also explain the heterogeneity seen in numerous cancers. Hakomori and Kannagi postulated that there are two main mechanisms for expression of tumor-associated carbohydrate antigens, specifically, incomplete synthesis (truncated glycans; Tn, sTn) and neosynthesis [de novo expression; sialyl Lewis a (sLea) and sialyl Lewis x (sLe x)][4]. Recent studies support the involvement of CSCs in tumor development, metastasis, chemoresistance, and recurrence[5] CSCs or tumor-initiating cells are the rare, small subset of cells in the tumor with the ability to give rise to complete tumor masses[5]. CSCs can self-renew, can undergo asymmetric or symmetric cell division, and areassociated with cellular heterogeneity. Theyare thought to be derived from mutations in the stem or progenitor cell and hence tend to have the same stem cell markers[5] and various CSC markers are defined in many cancers to identify and isolate CSC populations. Research has exploited membrane glycoproteins (CD44, CD24, ESA, CD133, etc.) to identify and sort CSC populations by using fluorescent antibody labeling and fluorescence activated cell sorting[4]. Another well-known method for isolating CSCs is Hoechst staining, the method by which cells are analyzed and sorted according to their ability to efflux the 33342 dye out of the cell. CSCs efflux the Hoechst dye due to higher levels of ABC transporters and appear as side populations (SP) in

Hoechst red versus Hoechst blue plot in flow analysis. In recent years, researchers worldwide have accepted the existence of CSCs mainly because of tumor heterogeneity, chemoresistance, and tumor relapse. Present available drugs are efficient in only killing the bulk of tumor mass, sparing CSCs and leading to tumor recurrence and metastasis.

2. GLYCOSYLATION'S ROLE IN CANCER

Glycans are vital in the cell biology of many cancers. They are responsible for tumor cell dissociation, metastasis formation, cellematrix interaction, angiogenesis, immune escape, cell signaling and communication, among other things[2]. Tumor cells often display glycosylation alterations especially in cancer types such as lung cancer and glioblastoma (GB)[3] in fact, it is the over expression of certain proteoglycans that characterize certain cancers[7]. Alteration of the serglycin proteoglycan has been linked to promoting progression and metastasis in triple-negative breast cancer, and heparan sulfate proteoglycan alterations have been implicated in colorectal cancer[8]. Proteoglycans can control the activation of such tyrosine receptors such as MET (hepatocyte growth factor receptor), EGFR (epidermal growth factor receptor), and IGF-1R (insulin growth factor receptor). In fact N-glycans are often covalently linked to asparagine (asn) and receptors that are involved in oncogenesis, for instance, IGFR and EGFR tend to have more N-glycan sites[2]. Ogata et al. corroborate this in a study which found that malignant cells had more N-linked sugar chains than normal cells .The relationship of cancer to N-linked glycosylation has sparked much research into inhibiting that pathway in the hopes of curtailing cancer progression. Further studies into the implications of N-linked glycosylation in cancer show that increase branching of B1-6 is correlated with metastasis. Moreover, the B1,6-N-acetylgluco-saminyltransferase V (GnT-V) is responsible for cancer cell invasion and migration[9]. N-linked glycosylation is by no means the only form of glycosylation that is tied to cancer. Abnormal expression of the O-glycosyltransferase enzymes is associated with multiple cancers, including lung and pancreatic types[10]. Park et al. in 2010, showed that enzymes associated with the O-linked pathway can lead to the development and progression of breast cancer[11]. They also found that the expression of GALNT6 an enzyme associated with O-linked glycosylation has been shown to glycosylate the mucin 1 (MUC1) oncoprotein, which contributes to carcinogenesis by interfering with B-catenin and E-cadherin. The group postulates that enzymes such as GALNT14 and GALNT6 could serve as predictive biomarkers in the fight against cancer[11]. The expression of truncated O-glycan structures has been linked to tumor cell epitopes and metastatic ability in cancers ranging from the colon, stomach, pancreas and lung[12,13]. O-linked and N-linked oligosaccharides are major components of mucins and multiple mucin domains regulate components of the tumor microenvironment, which tie into glycosylation's role in tumor immunity[14]. Last, but certainly not least, altered lectins and their relationship to glycans also have been shown to induce cancer development and proliferation. Tumor-associated glycans are dependent on lectin binding[9]. For example, galectins, such as galectin-1 (Gal-1) induce T-cell apoptosis causing angiogenesis and immunosuppression in several cancers such as melanoma, neuroblastoma, and lung cancers .Furthermore, selectin ligands are associated with mucins such as MUC1, MUC2, and MUC4 and interactions with these selectins 4 can lead to metastases development[15,16]. Whether it be alterations in N-linked glycans, O-linked glycans, or lectins, there is an undeniable association between aberrant glycan structures and cancer.

3. PROTEIN GLYCOSYLATION[6]

Alterations in protein glycosylation are amongst the main molecular events accompanying oncogenic transformations in the gastric and colorectal tracts[14-16]. In fact, protein glycosylation is one of the most frequent, complex and plastic posttranslational modification of membrane-bound and secreted proteins[17]. Glycans play a key role in protein folding, trafficking and stability. Moreover, they mediate several cell functions, such as cell adhesion, migration and signaling, as well as modulate immune recognition and host-pathogen interactions[16,18-20]. Protein glycosylation results from the highly coordinated action of nucleotide sugar transporters and sugar biosynthesis pathways, involving glycosyltransferases (GTs) and glycosidases in the endoplasmatic reticulum and the Golgi apparatus. As such, several factors may influence glycan biosynthesis, namely the under or overexpression of glycosyl-transferases, the impairment of glycosyltransferases chaperone function, altered glycosidase activity, changes in the tertiary conformation of a given peptide or growing glycan and the availability of sugar nucleotide donors, cofactors and acceptor substrates[21,22].

The miss localization of glycosyltranferases throughout the secreting organelles also contributes to significant alterations in cancer-associated protein glycosylation patterns[23-25]. Two main classes of glycans can be found at cell-surface glycoproteins: i) O-glycans, being the most common O-glycan that is initiated in the Golgi by the attachment of a GalNAc residue to the hydroxyl groups of serine (Ser) or threonine (Thr) amino acids of a given polypeptide chain (forming the Tn antigen GalNAcα-Ser/Thr, the simplest form of O-glycosylation)[26]; ii) N-glycans, whose biosynthesis initiates in the endoplasmatic reticulum by the addition of an oligosaccharide chain to an asparagine (Asn) residue within consensus peptide sequences of Asn-X-Ser/Thr (X denotes any amino acid except proline)[27]. Less abundant forms of protein glycosylation include O-Fucosylation, O-GlucNAcylation, OMannosylation[16]. Protein glycan chains are often branched or elongated and may present sialic acids, Lewis blood group related antigens or ABO(H) blood group 4 determinants as terminal structures[28].

Other modifications may include phosphorylation, O-acetylation of sialic acids and O-sulfation of galactose and Nacetylglucosamine residues, thereby increasing the structural complexity of the glycophenotype[29]. In addition, protein glycosylation patterns do not obey a predefined template, as it is regulated by several factors at the cell and tissue level, promptly responding to physiological and pathological changes[16]. Given its key functional and biological role, alterations in protein glycosylation underlying oncogenic transformations decisively contribute to the development of more malignant characteristics, such as cell-cell adhesion impairment, enhanced migration and promotion of lymphohematogenous metastization[16,30-32].

Altered protein glycosylation has been also implicated in the activation of intracellular oncogenic pathways and immune escape, thereby favoring cancer-tolerogenic immune responses[33,34]. Particularly, advanced stage tumors often overexpress or promote the de novo biosynthesis of immature and truncated O-glycans, such as the Tn, sialylTn (STn), T and sialyl-T (ST) antigens, due to a premature stop of the extension of Oglycosylation[35-37]. Oversialylation and fucosylation of glycan chains are also frequently observed in cancer, including terminal antigens like the sialyl-LeA (SLeA) and sialyl-LeX (SLeX)[38-40].

Contrasting with the tumor, these structures are often absent or just moderately expressed in the corresponding healthy tissues, holding potential for selective targeted therapeutics[38]. In addition, many of the proteins carrying cancer-associated glycans may also be shed into the blood stream or other bodily fluids, facilitating non-invasive detection methods. Despite the key role played by glycosylation, clinically approved and novel targeted therapeutic approaches for gastric and colorectal tumors have mostly resulted from intense genomic, transcriptomic and proteomic studies. Moreover, few efforts have been devoted to whole glycome and glycoproteome characterization of gastric and colorectal tumors, mostly due to its intrinsic molecular complexity. This has significantly delayed the development and translation of glycan-based diagnostic and therapeutic solutions to clinical routine.

Recently, the simplification and standardization of glycobiology-based methods has provided powerful analytical tools to improve our understanding of glycosylation alterations on specific cancer-associated proteins. This review summarizes recent insights from innovative research on the 5 glycobiology of gastric and colorectal tumors. It emphasizes the O-glycome and glycoproteome, envisaging the identification of more specific cancer glycobiomakers and the development of innovative therapeutic strategies.

Furthermore, it comprehensively discusses the implications of combining glycosylation, large scale genomics, transcriptomics and metabolomics towards true precision medicine settings. Protein glycosylation in gastrointestinal cancer: Molecular mechanisms underlying the aberrant glycan biosynthesis Perhaps the most studied cancerassociated glycoepitopes in gastric and colorectal cancers derive from a premature stop in the elongation of protein O-GalNAc glycosylation[16,37,41]. These antigens have been classically termed as simple mucin-type O-glycans, reflecting the abundance of this type of glycosylation in mucins. Nevertheless, these type of glycans may be virtually found in any membrane bound and secreted protein expressing Oglycosylation sites. O-GalNAc glycans biosynthesis can be initiated by up to 20 polypeptide GalNActransferases (GalNAc-Ts), which are responsible by catalyzing the transfer of a N-acetylgalactosamine residue from UDP-GalNAc to the hydroxyl group of Ser or Thr, originating the Tn antigen (Figure 1)[42-44].

The different GalNAcTs present a cell and tissue-specific expression[45], showing distinct and partially overlapping peptide substrate specificities that are crucial for O-glycosites definition[46]. There have been reports of an increased density of O-glycans in gastric and colon tumors, resulting from an increased GalNAc-Ts activity in tumor cells compared to normal cells[20,47]. In most normal gastrointestinal cells, the Tn antigen is further elongated by core 1 β1, 3-galactosyltransferase (C1GalT). This reaction originates the core 1 or Thomsen-Friedenreich (T)-antigen (Galβ1-3GalNAc-Ser/Thr), in a process dependent on the functional chaperone COSMC (Figure 1)[48]. The initial GalNAc may be extended and originate the core 3, catalyzed by β-1,3-Nacetylglucosaminyltransferase 6 (β3Gn-T6). Core 3 may be further substituted with a GlcNAc residue by core 3 β-1,3-N-acetylglucosaminyltransferase (C3GnT), originating core 4 (Figure 1). On the other hand, core 1 may originate core 2, catalyzed by β-1,6-Nacetylglucosaminyltransferases (C2GnTs). Core structures are frequently further elongated and terminated with ABO and Lewis blood groups determinants, as depicted 6 in Figure 1.

The downregulation of β3Gn-T6 and C3GnT was shown to suppress metastasis in colon carcinoma, suggesting that core structures may play a key role in cancer progression[49]. C1GalT is often overexpressed in tumors, resulting in an accumulation of T antigens, which has been associated with disease progression, metastasis and decreased survival[20,38]. Early sialylation also decisively contributes to a premature stop in O-glycans extension, leading to an accumulation of immature sialylated structures such as sialyl-Tn (STn; Neu5Acα2-6GalNAcα-O-Ser/Thr), mostly due to the increased expression of sialyltransferases like ST6GalNAc1[37,50]. The overexpression of Tn and STn has been observed in both early and advanced stage disease, generally associated with poor outcome[51,52]. Notably, pre-malignant and early stage colorectal tumors overexpress the STn antigen[53-55] due to a reduction in O-acetylation of sialic acids[53,56,57] responsible for protecting colonic mucins from degradation by intestinal bacteria[58]. Nevertheless, the molecular mechanisms underlying these transformations are not yet fully understood. Other modifications occurring in sialic acids may include a substitution of Neu5Ac by non-human Neu5G from dietary sources[59].

Recently, high levels of Neu5Ac were associated with increased consumption of red meat and as a promoter of systemic inflammation and cancer[60]. Furthermore, several studies report an overexpression of the T antigen sialylated form in colorectal carcinomas[61], whose contribution to disease warrants in depth investigation. In addition, gastric and colorectal tumours present high levels of SLeA (NeuAcα2,3Galβ1,3[Fucα1,4]GlcNAc-R) and SLeX (NeuAcα2,3Galβ1,4 [Fucα1,3]GlcNAcR) as terminal epitopes of protein O-glycans[62,63], but also of N-glycans and glycolipids[64,65]. In fact, SLeA and SLeX have been found highly expressed in many solid tumors, including digestive track carcinomas, and their expression levels have been correlated with metastasis and poor survival in cancer patients[66-68].

These antigens are structurally related with Lewis antigen determinants LeA and LeX, resulting from the α2,3sialylation of Type 1 or Type 2 (lactosamine) chains, followed by either α1, 4 or α1, 3-fucosylation (structural details and biosynthesis depicted in Figure 1B). SLeA/X are specific ligands for E- and P-selectins in endothelial cells, thereby acting as regulators of the metastatic cascade by promoting the adhesion of malignant 7 cells to the endothelium (Figure 2)[69,70]. Selectin ligands are also thought to play a role in tumor growth, invasion, and angiogenesis[32,71,72]. SLeA/X elevation in O-glycans, has been mostly associated with C2GnT overexpression and consequently core 2 biosynthesis[62,63].

In N-glycans, SLeA/X overexpression may also be potentiated by the β1, 6-branching of N-glycans, followed by further elongation with polylactosamine, whose role in cancer has been recently revised by several authors[16,21]. In addition, the H. pylori-induced expression of a β1,3-GlcNAc transferase, responsible by the synthesis of Type1/2 chains precursors in glycolipids, drives SLeA/X accumulation and carcinogenesis in gastric tissues[73]. The overexpression of this enzyme was also observed in colonic cancer tissues[74]. Nevertheless, in normal gastric and colonic mucosa, both type 1 (Galβ1,3GlcNAcβ1-R) and type 2 (Galβ1,4GlcNAcβ1-R) glycan chains may coexist[75,76].

However, malignant transformations in the colon are frequently accompanied by a downregulation of β3GalT5[77] that synthesizes type 1 chains in epithelia, and a upregulation of β4GalT-I[78] and IV[79], leading to an increase in type 2 chains (precursor for SLeX)[76]. Importantly, the overexpression of SLeX/A antigens in gastric and colorectal cancers may also influenced by "incomplete" and "neo" biosynthesis of terminal Lewis-related antigens. Regarding incomplete biosynthesis, nonmalignant epithelial cells of the digestive tract predominantly express disialyl LeA (diSLeA), presenting an additional O-6 linked sialic acid in comparison to SLeA[80-82]. The diSLeA antigens act has ligands for lymphocyte inhibitory receptors Siglecs-7 and -9 expressed on monocytes and macrophages, thereby contributing to maintaining immunological homeostasis in digestive organs[83,84]. Epigenetic silencing of the α2,6-sialyltransferase encoding gene is thought to be amongst the main events driving the shift from di- to mono-sialylated LeA antigens in cancer[84].

These events ultimately contribute to impairment of normal recognition of cancer cells by lymphoid cells. On the other hand, while non-malignant colonic epithelial cells predominantly yield the sialyl 6-sulfo LeX, cancer cells often accumulate significant amounts of SLeX[85]. Two main mechanisms have been proposed for this alteration: i) decreased expression of intestine-specific GlcNAc-6-sulfotransferaseI GlcNAc6ST[86-88]; ii) downregulation of the sulfate transporter gene, which has also been implicated in enhanced cell proliferation[89]. Recently, the downregulation of B4GALNT2 and 8 consequent decrease in histo-blood group carbohydrate antigen Sda (GalNAcβ1- 4[Neu5Acα2-3]Galβ) levels was also found to drive SLeX overexpression in colonic tumours[90]. In addition, no significant alterations have been found in the transcript levels of different fucosyl and sialyltransferases involved in SLeX biosynthesis[91-93]. In summary, epigenetic changes such as DNA methylation and/or histone deacetylation significantly contribute to SLeX/A overexpresion, particularly during the early stages of disease[94].

In locally advanced tumours hypoxia also plays a key role in glycome remodeling and SLeA/X neosynthesis. Namely, oxygen shortage has been shown to act as a trigger for epigenetic silencing and transcriptional induction of several glycogenes[94-97] and alterations in glucose metabolic fluxes directly implicated with glycosylation pathways[98,99]. It is now consensually recognized that gastric and colorectal tumor overexpress truncated, sialylated and fucosylated O-glycans that favor disease progression and dissemination. In particular, glycome remodeling translates in the accumulation of simple-mucin type O-glycans and selectin ligands, which decisively contribute to disease outcome.

Despite significant advances in understanding the biological events driving these alterations, a significant amount of questions remain unanswered regarding biosynthesis pathways. Namely, most studies are target-driven, based on cancer cell models and/or small number of patients, lacking the necessary pan-omics approach, such asglycomics, (glyco) proteomics, glycogenomics/ transcriptomics, and metabolomics, to unravel the complex nature of cancer-associated glycosylation. Nevertheless, key structural and biological insights have been provided to address the context-specific nature of cancer-associated glycans and its clinical implications in large and well characterized patient samples. 3. Role of O-glycosylation and sialylated Lewis antigens in gastric and colorectal carcinogenesis and cancer progression Glycans play major roles during the process of gastric carcinogenesis, being particularly relevant for the gastric pathogen Helicobacter pylori infection.

Namely, H. pylori expresses cell-surface lipopolysaccharides carrying Lewis blood group determinants in mimicry of the host glycosylation patterns[100-102], which are considered essential for escaping immune response and maintaining asymptomatic 9 colonization[103]. Furthermore, the interaction between bacterial outer-membrane adhesins and host glycan receptors, including fucosylated type 1, LacdiNAc-motifs (GalNAcβ1-4GlcNAcβ1-) and sialylated-Lewis antigens, is a critical step for H. pylori colonization of the stomach niche[104-108]. LacdiNAc is a rare terminal structure in mammals but gastric MUC5AC has been shown to carry this terminal modification[109] and a GalNAc transferase (β1,4-N-acetylgalactosaminyltransferase III) present in human gastric tissue was demonstrated to biosynthesize the LacdiNAc epitope[110].

In contrast, α1,4-GlcNAc-capped O-glycan, which are synthesized by α1,4-Nacetylglucosaminyltransferase (alpha4GnT) and expressed by the deeper gastric glands, have been shown to present a natural antimicrobial activity[111,112]. This antibiotic effect has been attributed to inhibition of the cholesterol αglucosyltransferase enzymatic activity and therefore interfering with H. pylori cell wall biosynthesis and impairing bacterial growth[113-115]. Moreover, α1,4-GlcNAc expression has been shown to prevent gastric cancer by suppressing tumor-promoting inflammation[116]. Remarkably, the different stages of the gastric carcinogenesis pathway are accompanied by striking changes of the gastric cells glycosylation profile (Figure 2)[14]. While healthy mucosa expresses mainly neutral glycans, H. pylori infection and chronic inflammation promote de novo expression of negatively charged sialylated and sulfated glycans[73,117,118], thereby increasing bacterial adhesion to gastric cells.

Aberrant cell surface glycosylation is not exclusive of the initial gastric carcinogenesis stages, being also observed in pre-malignant conditions and constituting a marked feature of gastric carcinoma cells[14]. Moreover, the aberrant expression of simple mucin-type carbohydrate antigen structures in cancer cells has been widely reported and the extent of this expression has been correlated with the aggressive phenotype and invasive potential of various cancer types, including gastric and colorectal tumors[51,52,119-124]. Several studies directed to Tn and STn antigens indicated that these antigens are highly expressed in gastric carcinomas[31,37,52,122] as well as in poorly differentiated adenocarcinomas of the colon[61]. Furthermore, gastric cancer cells glycoengineered to overexpress the STn antigen presented a more aggressive phenotype[31].

This included decreased cell-cell aggregation, as well as increased extracellular-matrix (ECM) adhesion and migration, resulting in tumor cell invasion[31]. In addition, the 10 overexpression of T-synthase has been correlated with FGF-β-mediated activation of FGFR2, promoting colon cancer progression[47]. Some reports have also focused on evaluating the role of altered protein O-glycosylation in tumor cell apoptosis; nevertheless, the mechanisms through which these events take place are far from clear. For instance, alterations in the O-glycosylation of death receptors in colorectal cancer cells have been suggested to affect sensitivity to Apo2L/TRAIL by promoting ligand-induced receptor clustering and consequent caspase-8 activation[125].

Moreover, O-glycosylation inhibitors showed induction of apoptosis and downregulation of proliferation in colorectal cancer cells[126]. In addition, the T antigen is not expressed by the normal colonic mucosa[61,127], mostly due to masking by sialylation[128]. However it is present in most tumours[61,127] and significantly overexpressed in metastasis[129]. This antigen interacts with galectin-3 and is thought to play a key role in mediating homotypic aggregation of cancer cells[130,131], protecting cells from anoikis[131]. In addition, it may promote the galectin3 mediated docking of tumor cells to endothelial cells[132] favoring metastasis. Moreover, T expression by cancer cells induces galectin-3 expression by endothelial cells[133], reinforcing its role in disease dissemination. T antigen expression has also been found to mediate the induction proliferative signaling, mediated by c-Met and MAPK[134-136].

As outlined in the previous section, increased tumor cell sialylation has an important impact in cellular recognition, adhesion and signaling[14,16,137]. Particularly, SLeA and SLeX have been demonstrated to be highly expressed in many cancers, and their expression levels have been correlated with metastasis and poor survival in cancer patients[66,67]. The overexpression of SLeX in gastric carcinoma cells has been shown to induce c-Met activation and an invasive phenotype[32]. Furthermore, SLeA and SLeX have been demonstrated to be preferential ligands for selectins on activated endothelial cells, thereby playing a key role in the metastatic process[16,138-140]. These findings highlight the plethora of biological events mediated by altered glycosylation in cancer, and the need to invest in deciphering its role in cell invasion and metastization, which will certainly translate into novel and more effective therapeutics.

Diagnostic and prognostic implications of altered glycosylation in gastric and colorectal cancers Specific truncated O-glycans and SLeA/X have been shown to present different expression levels in neoplastic lesions, when compared with their normal counterparts[16]. Moreover, these alterations often associate with clinicopathological variables, such as lymph node metastasis, tumor stage and recurrence[122,123]. Furthermore, cancer-associated glycans are often shed into the bloodstream and can potentially be used for non-invasive detection[133,134]. In fact, glycosylated epitopes are widely used in clinical practice as non-invasive biomarkers for gastrointestinal cancer diagnosis and for monitoring disease progression. Moreover, these epitopes can be used as prognostic markers of gastrointestinal patients' survival after tumor surgery[22,134,135].

The screening of glycobiomarkers in patient samples presents limitations related to the organ specificity and sensitivity for cancer lesions of some glycoconjugates. Nevertheless, several clinically approved serological assays are currently used for the quantification of specific glycobiomarkers in the serum of patients with gastrointestinal cancer. These include carbohydrate epitopes (CA19.9 and CA72.4) but also heavily glycosylated glycoproteins such as the carcinoembryonic antigen (CEA) and alpha-fetoprotein (AFP), whose specific glycoforms may hold potential to improve non-invasive diagnosis and prognosis. 4.1. CA19.9 The expression of this highly sialylated structure is qualitatively and quantitatively altered in cancer cells. The CA19.9 test recognizes the sialylated terminal structure SLeA in O-glycoproteins, such as mucins, and in glycolipids.

This serological test is broadly used to monitor recurrence and response to therapy in gastric, colorectal, pancreatic and biliary cancer patients[133]. Particularly, CA19.9 is the most studied and validated tumor marker used to monitor pancreatic cancer patient's response to therapy every 1 to 3 months[112]. CA19.9 serum levels present more than 80% of sensitivity and specificity in diagnosis of pancreatic cancer symptomatic patients[136]. Furthermore, in gastric cancer, CA19.9 positivity before surgery is 12 considered a risk factor for gastric cancer recurrence[150]. In colon cancer, high levels of CA19.9 have a prognostic significance of decreased survival[151,152]. Despite these observations, there is limited application of this serological marker in gastric and colorectal cancer diagnosis due to to frequent false positives in patients with benign diseases[146,153]. However, it has been proposed that the diSLeA/ SLeA ratio may be used to reduce this limitation[140]. 4.2. CA72.4 Elevated expression of another sialylated O-glycan, the truncated STn antigen, can be detected by the serological assay CA72.4 in gastric and colorectal tumors[146,154,155].

The CA72.4 detection of STn in the serum of healthy individuals has been shown to be limited. However, STn detection was reported in individuals with precursor lesions of gastric cancer[111]. In gastric cancer, the detection of this marker can be used as an independent prognostic factor associated with aggressiveness, poor prognosis and tumor recurrence[143,145,157]. Nevertheless, the use of CA72.4 serological assay has also limited application for screening and diagnostic purposes. 4.3. CEA CEA is a glycoprotein expressed by various gastrointestinal tissues. The serological assay that detects this glycoprotein is commonly used in clinical practice to monitor therapy successes and to evaluate recurrence after surgery in colorectal cancer patients[112-113]. CEA levels are used in pre-operative conditions for tumor staging and treatment planning[117,118,119]. However, sensitivity limitations of the CEA serological assay prevent early stage disease detection[119]. Moreover, CEA increased levels in non-cancer-related patients excludes general population screening applications. Notwithstanding, CEA increased levels are associated with poor prognosis and decreased survival of colorectal cancer patients.

In order to monitor therapy response and metastization in stage II and III colorectal cancer patients, it is recommended the measure of CEA levels, after surgery, 13 every 3 months, during at least 3 years after diagnosis. Nevertheless, falsely elevated CEA levels should be taken into consideration during the first weeks of chemotherapy. Recent glycomic studies have demonstrated that tumor tissues express specific CEA glycoforms that can be exploited to improve the predictive potential of this biomarker. 4.4. AFP AFP is an albumin-related glycoprotein, present in fetal serum, commonly used as a glycobiomarker for liver diseases, including cancer[166,167]. Despite the high levels of this marker in hepatocellular carcinoma (HCC), it was also present in benign liver conditions. Importantly, only the fucosylated form of AFP (AFP-L3) is differentially detected in hepatocellular carcinoma, compared to benign liver diseases[170]. The use of this marker has been approved by FDA for early stage HCC diagnosis.

In summary, while classical cancer-associated glycans and abnormally glycosylated proteins offer an upfront approach for non-invasive disease follow-up, prognosis and response to treatment, they present significant limitations for early detection. Nevertheless, recent advances in high-throughput glycan analysis technologies (see novel glycomic and glycoproteomic strategies below) contributed to glycoproteome characterization and consequent discovery of several new putative glycobiomarkers for gastric and colorectal cancers[41]. Namely, STnexpressing plasminogen glycoforms have been advanced as specific serological markers of gastric carcinoma precursor lesions and gastric carcinoma[41,119], which now warrants clinical validation. In addition, a comprehensive array of abnormally Oglycosylated mucin-derived glycopeptides has been used for seromic profiling of colorectal cancer patients. Autoantibodies have been identified to a set of aberrant glycopeptides derived from MUC1 and MUC4, with a cumulative sensitivity of 79% with a specificity of 92%[14].

Such approach demonstrates the potential of glycanmediated humoral responses in the diagnostic context as well as a tool for identification of abnormally glycosylated proteins, as demonstrated by us for esophageal tumours[120]. Altogether, these early studies have decisively 14 demonstrated that abnormal glycosylation holds a tremendous opportunity to improve on the specificity and sensitivity of classical cancer biomarkers and may provide novel glycotargets. It is now time for the glycobiomarker discovery field to evolve from the proof-of-concept studies towards comprehensive clinical settings.

It will also be important to take into consideration the complex and multifactorial nature of the diseases. As such, the combination of multiple biomarkers of different molecular natures will likely translate into more accurate diagnosis and predictive models. 5. Novel glycomics and glycoproteomic strategies for biomarker discovery in cancer Combining molecular information from glycan and peptide moieties holds tremendous potential for designing highly specific targeted therapeutics.

However, the fact that glycan structures do not obey to a predefine template, but are rather the result of the highly regulated action of several glycosyltransferases rapidly responding to microenviromental and physiological stimuli, presents a significant analytical hurdle. Nevertheless, glycomics-based chromatography and mass spectrometry (MS) methods have reached a standardization stage, providing highly sensitive analytical tools for precise mapping of the glycome[121,122]. Common analytical workflows begin with the selective release of the N-glycans from the protein backbone by PNGase F treatment, followed by the chemical release of the O-glycans by reductive βelimination[123].

While N-deglycosylated proteins may be directly identified by MS, the significant peeling of the protein backbone derived from chemical Odeglycosylation makes protein identification difficult. Then, glycans are often separated by liquid chromatography (LC), using nano dimension columns capable of high-resolution separations of minute amounts of complex glycan mixtures (nanofentomnole) in a single run prior to MS analysis[124,125]. Labeling glycans with fluorophores, namely 2-aminobenzamide, anthranilic acid or 2-aminobenzoic acid, has also provided a valuable tool for quantitative approaches by LC, being also compatible with downstream MS analysis[178].

Furthermore, chromatographic methods as well as tandem MS experiments have provide means to distinguish highly complex isomeric glycans, a determinant step to establish accurate structure-function relationships[126,127].

Despite these observations, few studies have comprehensively addressed the 15 glycome of gastric and colorectal tumors. Regarding gastric cancer, emphasis has been given to screening the patients' serum, envisaging tumor biomarkers for non-invasive detection[41,132]. Contrastingly, most studies regarding colorectal cancer have focused on tumor and cell lines analysis. These preliminary approaches consensually highlight significant alterations in both N- and O-glycosylation of cancerassociated proteins. A comprehensive glycomic characterization of larger sets of well characterized patient samples are now needed for translation to clinical settings. Glycomic studies are of key importance for the identification of abnormally glycosylated proteins and for precise glycosite assignment. Nevertheless, significant analytical difficulties arise from the high molecular heterogeneity and low concentration of these species in biological milieus.

As such, most glycoprotemic workflows comprehend a pre-enrichment step, using lectin affinity chromatography or immunoprecipitation with glycan-specific monoclonal antibodies (Figure 3)[126,127]. Likewise, the enrichment of sialylated glycoproteins by TiO2 affinity has also been successfully applied for identification of serum glycoproteins associated with gastric pre-malignant and malignant lesions[122]. The proteins are then digested to peptides with trypsin or other proteolytic enzymes and analyzed using standard proteomics. Nevertheless, densely glycosylated peptide domains may resist to proteolytic cleavage, hampering their identification by conventional MS approaches. Frequently, protocols include an enrichment step for glycopeptides carrying the glycans of interest, prior to nanoLC tandem MS analysis, facilitating glycosite mapping. The development of highresolution orbitrap mass spectrometers and the combination of Higher-energy C-trap dissociation (HCD) with Electron-transfer dissociation-type (ETD) fragmentation has enabled the simultaneous and precise characterization of glycan structures and glycosites, significantly boosting glycoproteomic studies[19,20] (Figure 3). Much effort has also been put in the development of genetically engineered cancer cell models expressing simple and homogeneous O-glycans, mimicking the Oglycosylation found in solid tumor[31,51,53,54].

In particular, the recent SimpleCell technology approach, exploring zinc-finger nucleases to knockout of COSMC gene, has been applied in a number of different human cancer cell lines, including colorectal cancer cells[192,193]. This allowed a precision mapping of the human OGalNAc glycoproteome, which revealed over 6000 glycosites in more than 600 O- 16 glycoproteins, mostly from the cell surface, greatly expanding the view of the Oglycoproteome and its functional role[128]. More recently, our group as applied a similar glycoproteomic strategy to the characterization of the wild type gastric cell line (KATO III), which naturally expresses partially truncated O-glycans, and two gastric cancer SimpleCells (AGS, MKN45)[41]. Over 499 O-glycoproteins and 1236 O-glycosites where identified in gastric cancer SimpleCells, and a total 47 O-glycoproteins and 73 Oglycosites in the KATO III cell line. The same study led to the identification of 28 STnglycosylated proteins in the serum of gastric patients that were absent from healthy individuals. Two identified candidate O-glycoprotein biomarkers (CD44 and GalNAc-T5) were further validated in gastric cancer tissues using immunofluorescence and proximity ligation assay[41]. In particular, this technique allowed the simultaneous detection of the glycan and the protein moieties, holding tremendous potential in clinical samples screening[41,129,130]. These strategies provided crucial information on the whole O-glycoproteome and brought light into a particular set of Oglycoprotein candidates with biomarker potential in gastric cancer. It is expected that these analytical and technological advances can be merged towards their application in future clinical settings.

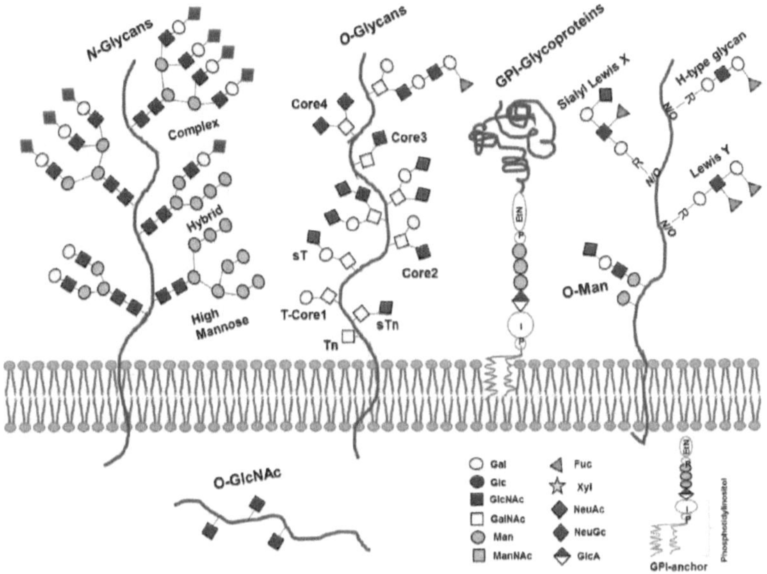

Pluripotency and reprogramming are regulated by O-GlcNAc modification of pluripotency-associated core proteins in embryonic stem cells (ESCs)

4. GLYCOSYLATION AND TUMOR IMMUNE EVASION

The immune system is a powerful testament to evolution and its ability to hone and perfect a system over time. The research advocated by Burnet and Thomas, researchers in the field of immuno-oncology see cancer as a failure of immune surveillance, or more accurately, the point where a tumor develops a microenvironment that is tolerant and can withstand the onslaught of our adaptive and innate immune systems[17]. Preclinical research conducted by that Pashov et al. group has revealed that glycosylation has an important role to play in cancer's ability to circumvent this immune surveillance. Studies have shown that aberrant glycan structures and truncated precursors or final structures of glycosylation prevent effective immune response; furthermore, tumor-associated carbohydrate antigens (TACAs) notoriously do not elicit strong adaptive immune response many of them boast immunosuppressive properties[18]. Some examples of N-linked glycans that subvert antitumor immune responses are Tri-antennary and Tetra-antennary, which both upregulate the b1,6 and MGATS enzymes, leading to inactivation of CD4þ T cells and macrophages[19]. Studies by Kannagi et al. found that the glycan structure Poly-N-Acetyllactosamine chain shows increased upregulation in b 1,6, MGATS, and upregulation in the O-glycan enzyme Core 2GnT, both of which lead to resistance against natural killer (NK) cells and promote metastatic disease[20].

Interestingly, research conducted by the Carrascal et al. group found that the O-linked glycan structures of Tn and Sialyl-Tn downregulated b 1,4, Gal-T, and COSMC in bladder cancer, which lead to tolerogenic phenotypes in innate and adaptive immune cells and enhanced antiinflammatory cytokine production[21]. Another glycan structure linked with cancer immune evasion is that of Sialyl-Le, which upregulates a-1, 3 and Fuc-T III, which leads chiefly to rejection of NK cells and promotes lung tumor formation[22]. As one can see, many studies have shown that alterations in glycan structures are often accompanied by the expression of cancer antigens that help tumors evade the immune system.

There is also mounting research into the effects lectin alterations may have on the adaptive immune response. Another aberrant mutation in O-linked glycosylation that affects the antitumor immune response is that of GalNAc. In a study conducted by Madsen and colleagues, the effect of GalNAc O-glycosylation was observed with an OVA-MUC1 model that contained peptides loaded onto dendritic cells (DCs) cocultured with interleukin-2[23]. Mice were inoculated with either nonglycosylated or GalNAc-glycosylated MUC1. It was found that the GalNAc-glycosylation group showed inhibition of major histocompatibility complex I (MHC I) and inhibited completely MUC1-specific CD8þ T-cell responses. Thus, the researchers concluded that aberrant mutations in O-linked glycans are implicated in some cases of blocking antigen presentation to CD8þ T cells[23]. Not just mutations in O-linked glycans cause immune trouble; aberrant N-linked glycan structures are equally culpable. With the advent of immune checkpoint inhibitors and the ever-growing field of immuno-oncology, there has been increasing investigation into glycosylation's effect on certain key receptors such as PD-L1. Recently, Li et al. in 2016 presented findings that the immunosuppression activity of PD-L1 was highly regulated by N-linked glycosylation. They found that GSK3b-mediated PD-L1 degradation by tyrosine kinase inhibitors can enhance antitumor immunity by reducing PD-L1 expression on cellular membranes[19]. Through testing T cell mediated cancer killing in vitro, the group observed massive cancer cell death showing that PD-L1 immunosuppression is dependent on glycosylation and may require it [19]. This understandably points to a new therapeutic strategy especially as physicians and scientists alike look to combinatory therapies with several immune drugs to help patients better respond to treatment. The key might be to combine these drugs with glycosylation inhibitors to create a more immune-hospitable tumor microenvironment.

FUNCTION IN STEMNESS

5. Stem Cells and Glycosylation

Stem cells are undifferentiated cells that can convert into differentiated and specialized cell types. Two of the most critical features of the stem cells are pluripotency and self-renewal[24]. Stem cells are usually identified and sorted by the specific markers expression, and these markers may be cell surface or intracellular proteins, transcription factors, enzymes, etc.[25]. The role played by glycosylation in the embryonic development has been studied. Yan et al. have demonstrated O-fucosylation of Notch receptors to control blood lineage commitment[26]. In another study by Seth et al., they have demonstrated that core O-fucosylation of apolipoprotein B is required for proper midline patterning during zebrafish development by modulating the sonic hedgehog signaling[27]. These studies display the significance of glycosylation in mediating the embryonic development process.

6. ESC Markers and Its Glycosylation Variation

Many of the pluripotency-associated markers of ESCs are known to be glycoproteins or glycolipids, namely, TRA-1-60 and 1-81 and, stage-specific embryonic antigen 3 and 4. The glycans of these markers could be the potential modulator of pluripotency and stemness, which need to be explored in detail[28,29]. A recent study by Jang H and colleagues has demonstrated the importance of glycosylation in regulating cellular pluripotency and reprogramming by modulating the core pluripotency-associated stem cell transcription factors in mouse ESCs . This study also demonstrated that specific O-GlcNAc modification of pluripotency markers Oct4 and Sox2 occurs in the undifferentiated mouse ESCs and this glycan modification is lost upon differentiation. The O-GlcNAc modified Oct4 shown to enhance its transcriptional activity and regulate transcription of pluripotency-associated genes, resulting in maintenance of the pluripotent state of mouse ESCs and reprogramming of mouse embryonic fibroblasts. The significance of glycosylation and glycan modification of stem cell transcription factor in regulating pluripotency in human ESCs and CSCs needs to be addressed.

7. Adult Stem Cell (ASC) Markers and Its Glycosylation Variation

Adult stem cells replace cells upon injury and maintain the tissue homeostasis, and it is not clear whether all the tissues of the body contain stem cells[30]. The role played by glycosylation in the maintenance of stemness in ASC has been studied. ESC marker LeX (SSEA-1) is shown to express specifically on adult mouse neural stem cells (NSCs)[31]. Expression of LeX antigen is identified on both glycolipid and glycoproteins and is shown to regulate the function of neural precursors cells[32]. Yagi and colleagues have demonstrated that N-glycans modified with LeX to regulate mouse NSCs through modulating Notch signaling. Authors have shown that undifferentiated NSCs express the higher amount of LeX carrying N-glycans compared to differentiated cells and are controlled by pax6 via upregulation of FUT-9 levels[33]. A detailed report on the role of glycosylation in stemness and differentiation of NSCs has been reviewed[34]. Hamouda et al. have characterized the N-glycans profile of undifferentiated and adipogenically differentiated in human bone marrow mesenchymal stem cells (MSCs). They have shown that N-glycans H6N5F1 and H7N6F1 are significantly higher expressed in undifferentiated than differentiated MSCs and identified as potential candidate markers[35].

In another study, CD44 modified SLeX glycans on MSCs showed to facilitate their trafficking to bone[36]. A cell surface marker, CD133 is expressed and identified as a stem cell marker in hematopoietic stem cells (HSCs), progenitor cells, NSCs, and prostate stem cells[37–39]. The role of CD133 glycosylation is described in the glycosylation of CSC markers section. Another cell surface marker, CD44, is also identified as a stem cell marker of HSCs[40] and the importance of its glycosylation is described in the glycosylation of CSC markers section.

8. Glycosylation and Self-Renewal Pathways

Self-renewal is an essential phenomenon in which stem cells divide to give rise to more stem cells and maintain the undifferentiated state. Maintenance of self-renewal is attributed to the activation of many signaling pathways like leukemia inhibitory factor (LIF)/signal transducer and activator of transcription (STAT3), bone morphogenic protein 4 (BMP4)/Smad, Wnt/β-catenin and fibroblast growth factor 2 (FGF2), and activin/nodal in mouse ESCs and human ESCs[41]. Studies have shown the significance of glycosylation in the regulation of self-renewal pathways in ESCs. Sasaki et al. demonstrated that specific cell surface glycan LacdiNAc (GalNAcb1-4GlcNAc) contributes to self-renewal of mouse ESCs by regulating LIF/STAT3 signaling. Authors in this study showed that B4GalNAcT3 mediated LacdiNAc expression on LIFR and gp130 is required for induction and maintenance of self-renewal in undifferentiated mouse ESCs[42]. In another study, self-renewal and pluripotency of mouse ESCs are known to be regulated by cell surface proteoglycan heparin sulfate (HS). RNA interference-mediated knockdown of HS chain elongation resulted in the loss of self-renewal and differentiation of mouse ESCs. They also showed that HS regulates the expression of Nanog through auto/paracrine Wnt/β-catenin signaling[43].

Multiple studies have shown that HS is required for lineage commitment of ESCs and to modulate pluripotency[44]. Ligands involved in the activation of self-renewal pathways are known to be modified with glycosylation. Glycan modification of Wnt3a is required for its active form production and in turn activation of β-catenin– dependent Wnt signaling[45]. N-linked glycosylation of FGFR1 is shown to regulate its binding to ligand and co-receptor HS and, FGF signaling[46].

9. GFs in Stemness of CSCs

Expression of a specific set of glycogenes at a time in a particular cell type determines the resultant signature of glycome on protein or lipid molecules. The different glycans on the cell membrane drive the diverse cellular signaling. Expression of glycogenes, specifically GFs, has been linked to the development and progression of many cancers[9]. One well-studied GF for the stemness of CSCs is glucosylceramide synthase (GCS). GCS is highly upregulated in breast, colon, leukemia, and various drug-resistant cancer cells. GCS catalyzes ceramide glycosylation, the rate-limiting step in glycosphingolipid synthesis. Reports have shown that inhibition of GCS sensitizes cancer cells to anticancer drugs and eliminates CSC population by modulating gene expression, reducing MDR1 and restoring expression of p53 via RNA splicing[128].

In breast CSCs, increased expression of ceramide glycosylation and globotriosylceramide (Gb3) was observed with the overexpression of GCS. This higher level of Gb3 was also shown to upregulate FGF-2, CD44 expression and Oct4 and to maintain stemness of breast CSCs through c-Src/β-catenin signaling. Silencing of GCS was also shown to disrupt Gb3 and kill breast CSCs[129] (Figure 5A). Liu YY and colleagues reported that inhibition of GCS led to increased ceramide levels in cells and restoration of the expression of wildtype p53 resulting in activation of p53-dependent apoptosis[130,131]. Liu's group has also shown that inhibition of GCS led to the expression of wild-type p53 and that it abolished the p53 R273H mutant-derived EMT and induced pluripotency of colon cancer[132] (Figure 5A). β1,4-N-acetylgalactosaminyl-transferase III (B4GALNT3) is overexpressed in the colon CSCs, which is involved in the synthesis of LacdiNAc structures.

A study indicated that LacdiNAc structures play a role in the self-renewal of mouse ESCs[42]. B4GALNT3 was reported to modify N-glycans of

EGFR with LacdiNAc and regulates stemness, migration, and invasiveness of CSCs. The knockdown of B4GALNT3 also decreased expression of the stem cell markers OCT4 and NANOG in colon cancer cells[133] (Figure 5C). Another GF, MGAT5 (GnT-V), is also shown to promote tumor development in many cancers, including colon carcinoma[9]. MGAT5 synthesizes N-glycans with β-(1,6)-branching and is involved in the development of many tumors by the way in which it modulates the function of various cell surface receptors and their intracellular signaling pathways[9].

In colon CSCs, MGAT5 was shown to modify the Wnt receptor, FZD-7, with β-(1,6)-branched N-glycans, thus affecting Wnt signaling, CSC compartments, and tumor progression[134]. Reduced colon (intestine) CSC populations in NOD/SCID mice were also interrelated with lower levels of MGAT5. Significantly reduced adenoma size and survival of MAGT5 knockout APCmin/+ mice were also observed in the study[134] (Figure 5C). Pancreatic CSCs were reported to overexpress the enzymes involved in the synthesis of fucosylated glycans such as fucosyltransferases (Fut1-4), GDP-fucose synthetic enzymes (FX, GMDS), and GDP-Fucose transporters[135]. In this study, authors reported an increase in the expression of α1,2- and α1,3-/α1,4-ucosylated glycans by lectin array[135]. In pancreatic and ovarian cancer, ST6Gal-1, which addsα2-6 sialic acid on substrate glycoproteins, is shown to confer CSC phenotypes by regulating the stem cell transcription factors Sox9 and Slug and to augment tumor-initiating potential and resistance to gemcitabine[136] (Figure 5B).

In bladder CSCs, GALNT1 has been shown to regulate the self-renewal and maintenance of bladder CSCs (BCMab1+CD44+) and bladder tumorigenesis by modifying O-linked glycosylation and activating SHH signaling through Gli1. Inhibition of bladder tumor growth was also observed by the intravesical instillation of GALNT1 siRNA and cyclopamine, an SHH inhibitor[137] (Figure 5D).

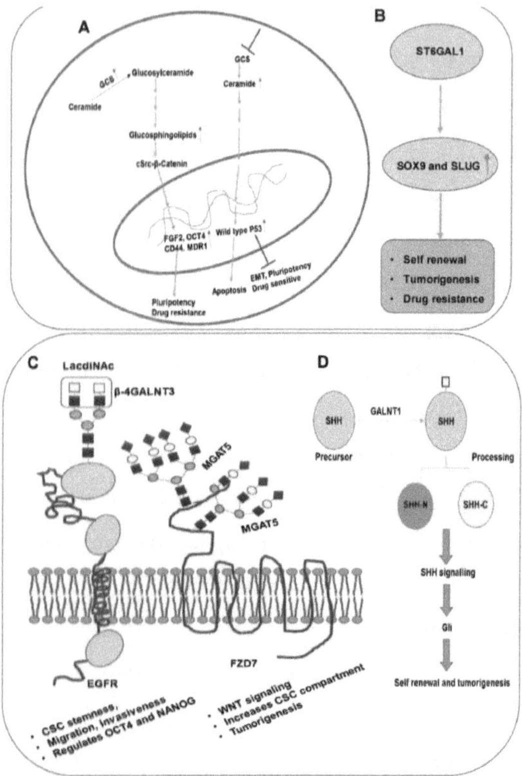

Figure 5. GFs regulating stemness in CSCs. (A) Glucosyl ceramide synthase regulates pluripotency and drug resistance through cSrc-β-catenin signaling. (B) ST6GAL-1 regulates stemness and drug resistance by inducing expression of SOX9 and SLUG. (C) B4GALT3 regulates stemness by inducing expression of OCT4 and NANOG by modifying EGFR with LacdiNAc. MGAT5 regulates stemness and tumorigenesis by modifying WNT receptor with β-1-6 branched N-linked glycans. (D) GALNT1-mediated modification of GalNAc on SHH induces expression of gli1 and regulates stemness and tumorigenesis.

FUNCTION IN TUMORIGENESIS

10. Glycosylation and Epithelial-Mesenchymal Transition

(EMT) in Cancer EMT is a remarkable phenomenon, which was initially observed to play a significant role in embryonic development and organ formation[47]. In the process of EMT, cells lose apical to basal polarity, change into fibroblastic nature, and display reduced epithelial markers and increased mesenchymal markers[47]. Several lines of research show the involvement of EMT in pathogenesis, particularly in tumor metastasis[48,49]. The importance of glycosylation in regulating the EMT and cell migration process has been studied. Guan and colleagues have demonstrated decreased expression of GSLs, Gg4, and/GM2, and Gg4 synthase was observed in TGFβ-induced EMT process in mouse and human epithelial cells[50,51]. Research by Freire-de-Lima and colleagues showed a direct correlation of O-glycosylation in regulating EMT process in human prostate epithelial cells. Authors have demonstrated TGFβ treatment to induce the expression of oncofetal fibronectin (onfN), GALNT-3, and GALNT6 activity and, in turn, O-glycosylation of onfFN resulting in the induction of EMT process[52]. A systemic review by the same author has been published on the importance of aberrant glycosylation in cancer cells undergoing EMT process[53].

Huanna et al. have demonstrated that GALNT14 regulates the cellular proliferation, migration, and invasion by inducing the expression mesenchymal EMT genes and by stimulating MMP-2 activity in breast carcinoma[54]. In another study, O-GlcNAcylation of GNB2L1 protein is shown to regulate the metastasis via modulating the EMT proteins translation in the chemoresistance of gastric cancer[55]. Lucena et al. demonstrated a link between EMT and altered glycosylation through activation of hexosamine biosynthetic pathway. The authors have shown that cancer cells uptake more glucose during EMT through hexosamine biosynthetic pathway activation and in turn induce aberrant cell surface glycosylation (sialylationα2-6, polyLacNAc, and fucosylation) and O-GlcNAcylation[56]. Role of specific O-glycan structures regulating the different function in tumor metastasis process has been reviewed. Tsuobai et al. have reported that core 2 O-glycans are helping in tumor metastasis by evading natural killer cells in circulation; in contrast, Core 3 O-glycans or O-mannosyl receptors suppress tumor metastasis by modulating integrin-mediated signaling[8]. Collectively, these studies display the significant role played by altered glycosylation in EMT and cellular migration process.

11. Glycosylation of CSC Markers

CSC markers are those molecules expressed at higher levels and used to identify and isolate CSCs from tumors[11]. CSC markers identified in numerous tumors are mainly cell surface glycoproteins, with the functional role of these glycan modifications being largely unknown[57].

CD44 and Its Glycosylation Variation: CD44 is a transmembrane glycoprotein that mediates lymphocyte homing and HA (hyaluronan)-dependent cell adhesion. The standard CD44 isoform (CD44s) is highly expressed in various cells types, including hematopoietic system. In contrast, the expression of variant CD44 isoforms (CD44v) is more limited. Both the standard and variant forms of CD44 actively contribute to the maintenance of stem cell populations by generating, embedding, and homing into a niche, establishing maintenance of quiescence and resistance to apoptosis[40]. Overexpression of CD44 in many tumors is implicated in tumor development[58], with CD44 identified as a universal CSC marker in many cancers, alone or with other markers such as CD24 and ESA[59].

The CD44 standard and its variants have been shown to be modified with N- and O-linked glycan modification. Moreover, the difference in the molecular weight of each isoform is linked to its differential glycosylation[60,61]. Bartolazzi et al. demonstrated that five potential N-linked glycosylation sites on CD44 are required for CD44-mediated adhesion to HA in human cell lines[62]. Glycosylation of CD44 has been shown to regulate HA binding in ovarian tumors[63]. It has also been shown that glycosylation of CD44 has both stimulatory and inhibitory effects on cell surfaces and soluble CD44 binding to HA in the Chinese Hamster Ovary cell line ldl-D[64].

The N-linked N-acetylglucosamine residue, O-linked glycans (N-deglycosylated), and N-acetylgalactosamine incorporation into non–N-linked glycans on CD44 are importantly shown to amplify the binding of cell surface

CD44 to HA. In contrast, α 2, 3- linked sialic acid on N-linked glycans inhibits CDD44 binding to HA[64]. Further studies showed that inhibition of N- and O-linked glycosylation of CD44 by tunicamycin (TM) and benzyl 2- acetamido-2-deoxy-α-D-galactopyranoside reduces the attachment of endometrial cells to peritoneal mesothelial cells[65]. Expression of sLeX glycans on CD44 in MSCs also facilitates their trafficking to bone[36] (Figure 2A). Expression of CD44 splice variants and their altered glycosylation are associated with metastatic properties of human tumors[58].

For instance, H-type glycan modification on CD44v6 produced by overexpression of the α1-2 fucosyltransferase gene resulted in increased tumor cell motility and tumorigencity in rat colon carcinoma cells[66,67]. Modification of T and sTn antigens (O-linked glycosylation) was also seen in CD44v but not CD44s in colon cancer[68]. Further, modification of the T antigen on CD44 was also seen in higher amount in lung, breast, and liver cancer–initiating cells[69]. In breast cancer– initiating cells, co-expression of fucosylated Histo-Blood Group Antigens, CD173 (H2), and CD174 (Lewis Y), and CD44 has been reported[15,70] (Figure 2A).

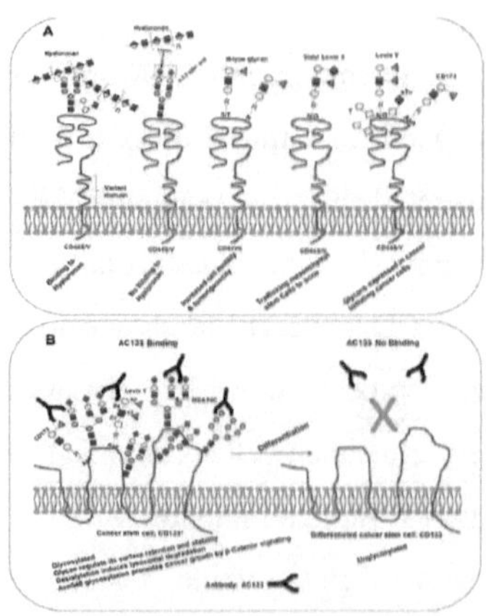

Figure 2. Glycan modification of CD44 and CD133. (A) Glycosylation of CD44 regulates its function in normal cells and cancer. N- and O-linked glycosylation of CD44 regulates HA binding. N-linked glycans with terminal α 2-3 sialic acid on CD44 inhibit binding to HA. H-type glycans on CD44v6 enhances cell motility and tumorigenicity. sLeX modified CD44 mediates mesenchymal stem cells trafficking to bone. CD44 in cancer-initiating cells is shown to express truncate glycans like Th, T, sT, and lewis Y and CD173. (B) CD133 glycosylation regulates its function in cancer and CSCs. N-linked glycans with α 2,3-sialic acids on CD133 regulates cell surface retention and stability, and desialylation induces its lysosomal degradation. N-linked glycosylation at Asn548 enhances tumor growth through β-catenin signaling

Importance of CD133 Glycosylation: CD133 (Prominin-1) is a cell surface marker that is expressed in HSCs and progenitor cell subpopulation but not in adult tissues[37]. Deregulated expression of this antigen was observed in several malignant hematopoietic diseases and in myelodysplastic syndrome. CD133 is widely used as a CSC marker in several malignancies[37]. Comparative genomics analysis on prominin-1 has shown that tandem TCF/LEF binding sites were conserved in PROM1 orthologs in human chimpanzee, mouse, and rat. The study proposes the involvement of CD133 in activation of WNT signaling in ESCs, adult, and CSCs[71]. Two monoclonal antibodies, AC133 and AC141, recognize glycosylated epitopes (undefined) of CD133 on the cell surface. These antibodies have been used to analyze and isolate CSC populations in many cancers, and a study demonstrated that, along with protein expression, the glycosylation status of CD133 may play a critical role in stem cell maintenance[72].

Further, studies showed that binding of AC133 is lost when CSCs differentiate and lose their stemness, but that this does not affect the change in mRNA and protein levels of human prominin-1[73] (Figure 2B). In the same year as this study, Zhou and colleagues showed α2,3-sialylation to regulate the stability of stem cell marker CD133 in NSCs and gliomainitiating cells. They reported that CD133 was modified with N-linked glycans, with the terminal via α2,3-sialylation and desialylation with neuraminidases accelerating its degradation through the lysosomedependent pathway[38]. AC133-negative glioblastoma cells have been shown to express a truncated prominin-1 variant protein, CD133, which is truncated with a molecular mass corresponding to ~16 kDa as detected by C24B9 (the anti-CD133 antibody) in the cytoplasm[74]. Another study demonstrated that N-linked glycan modification on CD133 regulated its cell surface localization and recognition by AC133.

Differential glycosylation of N-glycan modification profiles was observed between CD133+ and CD133− cells. Enrichment of biantennary complex-type glycans and increase in the high-mannose type and terminal α2,

3-sialylation (ST3GAL6 overexpression) of N-glycans in CD133+ cells were observed[75]. Hypoxia was shown to induce the expression of CD133 by upregulation of OCT3/4 and SOX2 through HIF alpha signaling in human lung cancer cells[76]. In another study, hypoxia was shown to enhance glycosylation of CD133 in GSCs, and it was hypothesized that hyperglycosylated CD133 helped survival and invasiveness in GSCs[77] (Figure 3A). Liu et al. characterized the glycan sites of CD133 and demonstrated that loss of N-glycosylation at Asn548 reduced prominin-1, promoted cell growth and its association with β-catenin, and in turn inhibited β-catenin signaling in liver cancer. N-liked glycosylation sites of CD133 identified by mass spectrometry analysis were Asn206, Asn220, Asn274, Asn395, Asn414, Asn548, Asn580, Asn729, and Asn730[78]. Co-expression of T anntigen and CD133 was seen in lung, breast, and liver cancer–initiating cells[69]. Coexpression of CD173 (H2) and CD174 (Lewis Y) with CD133 has also been reported in breast cancer–initiating cells[70].

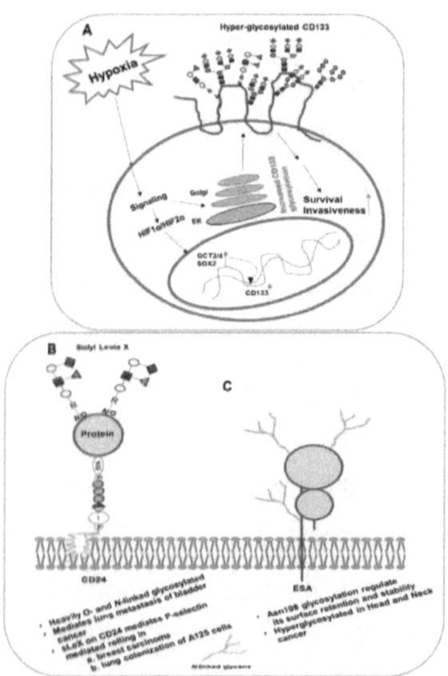

Figure 3. Glycan modification of CD133, CD24, and ESA. (A) Hypoxia enhances survival and invasiveness by inducing expression and hyperglycosylation of CD133 through Hif1α/Hif2α/OCT3/4/SOX2 signaling axis. (B) Glycosylation of CD24 mediates metastasis. CD24 is modified with N- and O-linked glycans. sLe^x modifies CD24-mediated, P-selectin-mediated rolling and lung colonization. (C) Glycosylation of ESA regulates its function in cancer. N-linked glycosylation at Asn198 on ESA regulates its surface retention and stability. ESA is hyperglycosylated in cancer compared to normal tissue.

Surface Marker CD24 and Glycosylation Variation: In mice, CD24 was discovered as a heat-stable antigen and identified as a marker to differentiate hematopoietic cells and neuronal cells[79,80] CD24 (B cell differentiation marker) is a cell surface glycoprotein linked to glycosylphosphatidylinositol, mainly expressed on human B cells and in many tumors. It consists of a small protein core of 27 aa's that are heavily glycosylated with N- and O-linked type of glycans[81,82]. Expression of CD24 was observed in higher levels in various human cancers and was involved in the cell adhesion, tumor progression, and metastasis[83–86]. CD24 was identified as a ligand for an adhesion receptor, P-selectin, on platelets and endothelial cells[87], through which it helps in extravasation of tumor cells in circulation. Further, CD24 increases tumor cell proliferation and it shows increased adhesion to fibronectin, collagen and lamin[84]. Cells expressing CD24+ are identified as CSCs in ovarian and colorectal cancers[88]. Myriad studies have shown vital role of CD24 in ovarian cancer metastasis, establishing it as a potential new CSC marker[89–92]. Gao et al. demonstrated that 5000 CD24+ cells form tumors in animal models with higher expression of stemness genes and found no tumorigenicity with the same number of CD24− cells[91]. Similarly, 500 CD24+ cells were shown to form tumors in mice models and express stemness genes, and were identified as CSCs in human nasopharyngeal carcinoma[93]. In another study, human ovarian cancer cell lines with phenotypes of CD44+CD24+EpCAM+ showed enrichment for stem/progenitor cells clonogenic capacity. A total of 0.5% to 1% of CD44+CD24+EpCAM+ cells were identified as CSCs in pancreatic cancer cells[94]. In contrast, CD44-high and CD24-low cells were identified as CSCs in breast and prostate cancer[95,96]. The importance of CD24 glycosylation in regulating its function in cancer has been studied. CD24 modified with sLe x was shown to meditate Pselectin–dependent rolling in breast carcinoma in vitro and in vivo[87]. CD24 with sLe x modification also mediates P-selection–

dependent rolling and lung colonization of human A125 adenocarcinoma cells[97]. CD24 further mediates the development of lung metastasis of bladder cancer[98] (Figure 3B), further showing the involvement of glycans on CD24 to mediate tumorigenesis and metastasis.

12. Role of Epithelial Cell Adhesion Molecule (EpCAM) in CSCs Maintenance and Glycosylation Variation

EpCAM or epithelial surface antigen (ESA) is amcell surface glycoprotein overexpressed in multiple tumors and in CSCs[99]. EpCAM promotes cell cycle and proliferation by upregulating the proto-oncogene c-myc and cyclin A or E[100]. EpCAM also regulates cellular metabolism by upregulating the fatty acid-binding protein E-FABP and contributes to carcinogenesis[101]. EpCAM is involved in the maintenance of hESCs in the undifferentiated phenotype by directly regulating few reprogramming genes, including c-MYC, OCT-4, NANOG, SOX2, and KLF4[102]. In contrast, one study identified EpCAM only as a surface marker to identify undifferentiated hESCs as silencing of this gene did not affect the levels of pluripotent marker[103]. EpCAM was shown to be Nglycosylated at the three-glycosylation sites: Asn74, Asn111, and Asn198 in human epithelial cells. In another study, EpCAM was shown to be N-glycosylated at Asn88 and Asn51 expressed in insect cells[99,104]. In head and neck cancer, EpCAM has been reported to be hyperglycosylated with N-linked glycans compared to autologous normal epithelia[105].

EpCAM hyperglycosylation at Asn198 regulates its protein stability and cell surface retention in HEK293 cells[106]. Furthermore, N-glycosylation of EpCAM has been shown to regulate apoptosis in breast cancer cells, as deglycosylation of EpCAM promoted apoptosis and inhibited cell proliferation of breast cancer cells[107] (Figure 3C).

13. CSCs and Mucins

Mucins are heavily glycosylated proteins carrying greatly O-linked glycans with few N-linked. O-linked glycosylation mainly takes place on serine, threonine, and proline-rich regions of variable tandem repeat regions of mucins. Mucin expression is commonly seen on epithelial cells, where they have primary protective functions against microbial infections [5, 108]. Deregulated mucin expression has been linked to the pathogenesis of many diseases, including cancer. Mucins such as MUC1, MUC4, MUC5AC, and MUC16 are some of the well-studied O-linked glycoproteins for tumor-promoting potential[109–113]. Aberrant glycosylation of mucins has been associated with cancer development and progression[5,9,114]. The role of mucins and their altered glycosylation in CSCs has not been explored. MUC1, a transmembrane glycoprotein, is overexpressed and aberrantly glycosylated in many cancers. MUC1 contains mainly core 2, its elongated glycan structures in normal cells; however, expression of truncated and neo-glycan structures is observed in cancer. This aberrant glycosylation of MUC1 activates oncogenic signaling in cancer[115]. N-terminal cleaved mucin 1 (MUC1) is expressed only in undifferentiated human pluripotent stem cells and mediates its growth by acting as a growth factor receptor[116].

MUC1 expression has been observed in the CD44+CD24+ESA+ and CD133+ CSCs of pancreatic cancer[117]. Overexpression of MUC1 has been reported in human stem cells fraction of cord blood cells and in many acute myeloid leukemia (AML) cases. MUC1 has been shown to increase frequencies of progenitor and long-term culture-initiating cells[118]. MUC1 overexpression is seen only in AML stem cells and not in normal stem cell counterparts; targeting of MUC1C by GO-203 has been shown to deplete AML in vivo[119]. Expression of the hypoglycosylated form of MUC1 expression was reported in the SP of MCF7 breast cancer cells[120]. MUC1 overexpression and

CD44+ / CD24− cancer stem-like cell enrichment were observed in response to exposure of tumor-associated macrophages to breast cancer MCF7 cells[121].

Apoptosis of MCF7 cells triggered by staurosporine has been shown to activate CD44+ /CD24− cancer stem-like cells by increasing expression of ESA and MUC1[122] (Figure 4A). Mucin 4 is also aberrantly expressed in many cancers and has been identified as a diagnostic cancer marker[114,123]. MUC4 maintains CSC population in ovarian cancer by stabilizing Her2 expression. Its overexpression increases the SP and CD133+ CSCs of ovarian cancer[124]. MUC4 overexpression also increases the CD133+ CSCs population of pancreatic cancer and was shown to provide gemcitabine resistance[125] (Figure 4B). Another transmembrane glycoprotein, MUC16 (CA125), a heavily glycosylated and large mucin, is implicated as having a tumor-promoting role in many cancers, including ovarian and pancreatic[110]. MUC16- expressing cells are identified as the source of CSCs in ovarian cancer.

Studies showed that only CA125+ /lineage− cells form tumors but not CA125/lineage cells in mouse orthotopic implantation[126]. In another study, the role of MUC16 in the enrichment of CSC populations and in tumorigenesis, and its metastatic potential in pancreatic cancer were demonstrated[110]. MUC16-cter mediates upregulation of stemness genes such as NANOG and LMO2 through JAK2 nuclear translocation and histone 3 phosphorylation, and it maintains stemness[127] (Figure 4C).

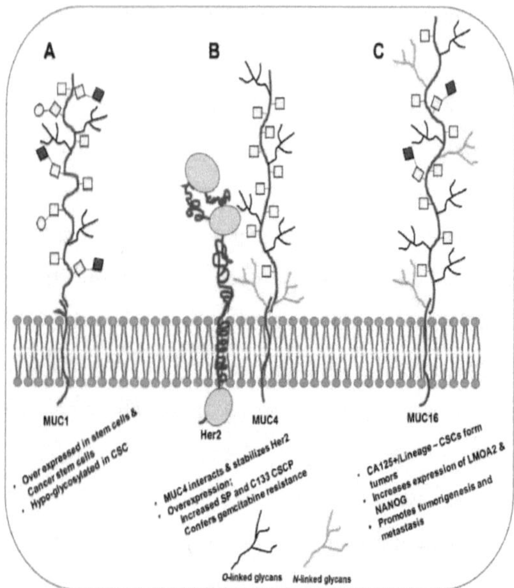

Figure 4. Role of mucins in CSCs. (A) Mucin 1 is overexpressed in human pluripotent stem cells and CSCs. Mucin 1 is hypoglycosylated in a CSC population. (B) Mucin 4 expression increases CSC population and provides drug resistance by Her2-mediated signaling. (C) Mucin 16 expressing cells identified as CSCs and Mucin 16 expression shown to regulate stem cell transcription factors LMOA2 and NANOG through the JAK/STAT pathway.

FUNCTION IN METASTASIS

14. Role of protein glycosylation in cancer metastasis

Metastasis is the multi-step process of hematogeneous, lymphatic or peritoneal spread of tumour cells, leading to secondary tumours. A metastatic tumour cell has to go through a series of essential events, including epithelial-mesenchymal-transition (EMT), detachment from the primary tumour mass, adherence to proteins of the extracellular matrix (ECM), migration on and degradation of ECM proteins, invasion into neighboring tissue, penetration into lymphatic or blood vessels, spreading into different parts of the body, and extravasation from the vessels to form a metastatic tumour. In this review, we will give an overview and describe recent results on the role of glycosylation in tumour metastasis, with view on O-glycans, N-glycans and glycosaminoglycans. We will concentrate on the influence of glycosylation on the above-mentioned steps of metastasis.

O-glycan:

2.1. Biosynthesis and types of O-glycans The O-glycosylation is a covalent post-translational modification in which monosaccharides are transferred to serine (Ser) and/or threonine (Thr) residues of specifific proteins by an Oglycosidic bond. The synthesis of O-glycans takes place in the Golgi apparatus and is mostly initiated by the activity of polypeptideGalNAc-transferases (pp-GalNAcTs, GALNTs) that link a single N-acetylgalactosamine (GalNAc) residue to Ser or Thr, thus forming the Tn antigen. In contrast to this glycan type which is termed mucin-type O-glycans, a wide range of non-mucin O-glycans exist, namely -linked O-fucose, -linked O-xylose, -linked O-mannose, -linked O-N-acetylglucosamine (O-GlcNAc), - or - linked O-galactose, and - or -linked O-glucose glycans. Since there are only limited data on the functional consequences of these modifications, they will not be further addressed in this review. By elongation of the Tn antigen, four core structures named core 1 to core 4 emerge depending on the monosaccharide types and sequence. Both, synthesis of **core 1** (also known as T antigen or Thomsen-Friedenreich antigen), catalysed via the glycosyltransferase C1GalT1 (T-synthase) and its chaperone COSMC, and **core 2**, which is formed through the action of the glycosyltransferase C2GnT, comprise galactose (Gal), whereas the latter has a −GlcNAc in addition (Fig. 1). The Tn antigen can be converted into **core 3**, containing one GlcNAc,followed by **core 4**, which includes two GlcNAc residues by the action of C2GnT and C3GnT. Further branching leads to more complex O-glycans including galactose, N-acetylglucosamine, fucose or sialic acid. The Tn and T antigens can be further sialylated creating sialyl-Tn antigen (via the alpha-2,6-sialyltransferase ST6GalNAcI) and sialylof disialyl-T antigen (via alpha-2,3-sialyltransferase ST3Gal-I and ST6GalNAcI), respectively. Beside the T and Tn antigens, certain Lewis antigens are often found in tumour tissues where they enable binding of tumour cells to selectins expressed by endothelial or blood cells[1] (Fig. 1). Sialyl-Lewisa (SLea) is synthesised by adding 3-Gal to GlcNAc via 3-Gal-transferase (3-GalT), followed by the addition of 3- sialic acid by 3-sialyltransferase (ST3Gal) and of 4-Fuc to GlcNAc by 4-Gal-transferase (4-FucT). In contrast, sialyl-Lewisx (SLex) is synthesised by the addition of 4-Gal to GlcNAc via 4-Gal transferase (4-GalT) closely followed by ST3Gal and of 3-Fuc to GlcNAc by 3-Fuc −transferase (3-FucT).

Which proteins are O-glycosylated?

Numerous proteins, including enzymes, transcription factors, receptors and structural proteins are regulated and/or modifified by O-glycosylation and this posttranslational modification has been implicated repeatedly in cancer[2]. Many cell-surface or secreted proteins carry mucin-type O-glycans, which protects them against proteolytic degradation but also modulates recognition, adhesion and cell-cell-communication functions.

Examples of O-glycosylated proteins are:

- Nuclear phosphoprotein c-myc which regulates cell proliferation, differentiation and apoptosis.
- Cell surface proteins like mucins MUC1, MUC2 etc., sialomucin, CD44, integrins and other cell adhesion proteins involved in cellcell-interaction, cell adhesion and migration.
- Structural proteins e.g. plakoglobin and -catenin modulating cell-cell-adhesion and downstream signaling pathways (for example Wnt/-pathway)
- C-type lectins (i.e. selectins) which also bind O-glycans
- Receptors e.g. death receptors to control sensitivity to proapoptotic signals

15. Glycans and metastasis

Tumour-specific alterations in glycosylation can result either in loss or in alteration of carbohydrate structures. The tumourassociated Tn antigen is highly expressed in more than 90% of breast tumours as well as 70–80% of colon, lung, bladder, cervix, ovarian, stomach and prostate carcinomas[3–5] and its presence is associated with high metastatic potential and poor prognosis[6,7]. In histochemical studies, O-glycan antigens are frequently analyzed by use of specific lectins: In example, Helix pomatiaagglutinin (HPA) specififically binds to Tn and peanut agglutinin (PNA) to core 1 and 2 structures. Binding of both lectins to breast cancer tissue has been shown to correlate with poor survival, lymphatic invasion and lymph node metastasis in breast cancer patients[8]. Tn and sTn antigen are often simultaneously synthesised and high levels of both promotes tumour growth and metastasis in vivo in breast and gastric tumours[9,10].

The T antigen influences adhesion of tumour cells to the endothelium due to its interaction with galectin-3 which drives metastasis[11,12]. The core 3 O-glycans also play a key role during malignant progression: In pancreatic cancer, core 3 structures are downregulated because of loss of functional core 3 synthase thereby modifying migration, invasion and metastasis[13]. SLe glycans bindto E- anP-selectins, whicharemainly expressed in endothelial and immune cells, thereby promoting extravasation[14]. Diverse studies in the last years suggest that tumour cells mimic the leukocyte adhesion cascade in order to extravasate. Here,sLE-selectin binding facilitates initial cell tethering and rolling which subsequently leads to fifirm cell adhesion, extravasation and metastasis[15,16].

16. Target proteins of O-glycosylation involved in metastasis

Mucins are highly O-glycosylated proteins and aberrant glycosylation of these structures has been implicated in cancer. In breast cancer O-glycosylation of mucin 1 (MUC1) regulated via C1GALT1 promotes MUC1-C/ß-catenin signaling which leads to tumour cell growth, migration and invasion in vitro as well as tumour growth in vivo[17]. In another study the glycosyltransferase GALNT6 has been showed to glycosylate and stabilise MUC1 driving carcinogenesis via disruption of -catenin- and E-cadherin-mediated cell adhesion[18] O-glycosylation of the cell-surface glycoprotein CD44 is frequently altered in tumour cells[19]. In colon carcinoma cells O-glycosylated CD44 can bind endothelial E-selectin, which in turns contributes to metastasis[20]. In breast cancer cells some CD44 glycoforms possess high shear-resistant selectin-binding activity due to O-glycan- and N-glycan-based sialofucosylated terminal carbohydrate groups, whereas other CD44 variants lack this activity[21]. Integrins are also O-glycosylated which inflfluences the attachment of tumour cells to the extracellular matrix (ECM) as well as cell-cell-interactions. In hepatocellular carcinoma cells, modification of integrin 1 via C1GALT1 regulates adhesion, migration and invasion and enhances metastasis in vivo[22]. Glycan binding proteins such as siglecs, galectinsand selectins are themselves glycosylated and are highly specific for certain sugar moieties. These proteins are associated with cell-cellrecognition, cell adhesion and motility. In prostate cancer--galactoside–binding protein galectin-4 affects the expression of E-cadherin modulating EMT, invasion and metastasis[23]. This effect is dependent on O-glycosylation mediated by C1GALT1. Osteopontin (OPN), also known as bone sialoprotein I, has a pivotal role in bone remodeling, inflflammation and cancer metastasis. Interestingly, OPN is highly O-glycosylated and its glycosylation status affects its phosphorylation and cell-adhesion activity[24].

17. Enzymes involved in O-N glycosylation and metastasis

Enzymes involved in O-glycosylation and metastasis: Overexpression or downregulation of glycosyltransferases and glycosidases affects the amount and pattern of glycans, influencing tumour progression and metastasis. The altered expression of glycosylation enzymes can be due to:

i) dysregulation at the transcriptional level,

ii) dysregulation of chaperone function or

iii) epigenetic mechanisms, i.e. methylation [25].

So far, 20 ppGalNAcTs (GALNTs) are noted and their under- or overexpression is frequently associated with tumour progression and metastasis. It has been shown for various tumours entities that the relocation of ppGalNAc-Ts from the Golgi to the ER promoted cell adhesion, cell motility and invasiveness[26].

GALNT1 was found to be frequently up-regulated in hepatocellular carcinoma and this was correlated with poor patient survival[27]. Knockdown of GALNT1 decreased cell migration and invasion via diminishing EGFR signaling. Interestingly, in the same tumour entity GALNT2 was downregulated which was associated with vascular invasion and recurrence[28]. GALNT2 overexpression decreased EGF-induced cell growth, migration and invasion in vitro and in vivo. In gastric adenocarcinoma low GALNT2-expression induces migration, invasion and metastasis in vivo[29] and is a prognostic marker for better patient survival in neuroblastoma. Here GALNT2 affects O-glycan structures of IGF-1R and thus triggers downstream signaling events [30]. In pancreatic tumours downregulation of GALNT3 leads to increased cell motility and adhesion to the tumour endothelium[31]. Knockdown of GALNT3 increases expression of ß-catenin and e-cadherin[32]. The expression of GALNT3 has been described as a potential diagnostic and prognostic marker for pancreatic and lung cancer[33,34]. C1GALT1 is overexpressed in hepatocellular carcinomas where its expression is associated with advanced tumour stage, metastasis and poor survival[35].

In experimental systems, C1GALT1 overexpression enhanced cell adhesion to ECM proteins, migration and invasion in vitro as well as metastasis in vivo. In breast cancer C1GALT1 is frequently up-regulated and promotes migration, invasion and growth of tumour xenografts via modulation of MUC1/ß-catenin signaling[17]. In our own recent study, high C1GALT1 protein or mRNA expression was associated with shorter disease-free survival in breast cancer patients, and its prognostic value was clearly increased if, in addition, either GALNT1, GALNT8 or GALNT14 was highly expressed, enabling synthesis of T antigens[8]. Several other enzymes are relevant for the synthesis of selectin ligands and thus for hematogeneous metastasis. GCNT1 (C2GNT1) and GCNT4 (C2GNT3) are involved in formation of core 2 structures which serve as carriers of Lewis antigens. In a study based on microarray data of 194 breast cancer samples, both enzymes showed a significant correlation to shorter survival, even in multivariate analysis, and an increased frequency of distant metastasis[36].

In the same study, the fucosyltransfrases FUT1 was associated with poor prognosis and distant metastasis, whereas the fucosidase FUCA1 was a favorable prognostic indicator and associated with a low percentage of lung metastasis. In experimental settings, FUCA1 reduces the invasive potential of breast cancer cells and their adhesion to selectins and endothelial cells under flow conditions[37]. An additional prognostic glycosylation enzyme in breast cancer is the sialyl transferase ST3GAL6 [8] which has been shown to promote migration and metastasis in various tumour types[38,39].

Further, the expression of ST6GalNAc-I,the major sialyl-Tn antigen synthase, correlates with invasion and metastasis. In hepatocarcinoma cells silencing of ST6GalNAc-I leads to tumour migration and invasion due to PI3K/AKT/NF-B pathway[40].

N-glycans

*Biosynthesis and types of N-glycans:*In contrast to O-glycosylation, N-glycosylation takes place during translation of target proteins by addition of glycan structures to the amino group of asparagine (ASN) residues at the consensus motif asparagine-X-serine/threonine (NXS/T) in which X is any amino acid except proline.Instead of step-by-step additionof single sugar residues, N-glycosylation starts with synthesis of a dolicholbound oligosaccharide precursor in the ER, consisting of 14 sugar moieties, among them 9 mannose residues. This oligosaccharide is then transferred to a suitable ASN residue within the nascent polypeptide by the oligosaccharyltransferase (OST) protein complex (Fig. 2). After this transfer, the correct folding and secretion of the glycoprotein depends on trimming of the glycan precursor in the Golgi, resulting in **high-mannose glycans**. Removal of part of the 9 mannose residues by Golgi mannosidases is the prerequisite of formation of **complex or hybrid** di-, tri- or tetraantennary **glycans** (Fig. 2). These can then undergo a variety of extensive modifications including sialylation, fucosylation, addition of galactose, GlcNAc etc., resulting in highly complex and heterogeneous structures. A specific modification is the addition of 1,4-bound GlcNAc to the beta-linked mannose of the trimannosyl core by MGAT3 resulting in the formation of "bisecting" N-glycans. Due to sterical features, this largely prevents further branching of the glycan.

Which proteins are N −glycosylated?

In humans, there are more than 2000 proteins harboring an amino acid motif suitable for N-glycosylation. These are either membrane-bound or secreted, but never cytoplasmic or nuclear proteins.

Examples of N-glycans are:

- Adhesion proteins including members of the immunoglobulin superfamily (ALCAM, ICAM1, BCAM etc.), CD44, integrins and cadherins,
- Secreted proteinases like kallikreins, cathepsins, carboxypeptidase E, matrix metalloproteinases, PSA etc.
- Receptors like EGFR, HER2/neu, TGFreceptor, IGF2R etc.
- ECM molecules like fibronectin, laminin etc.
- Wnt family members
- c-Kit, TIMP1, tetraspanins, clusterin etc.

N-glycans and metastasis:In human tumours, cancer-specifific N-glycan alterations include:

1. Premature termination of glycan processing, leading to accumulation of high-mannose glycans in the cells;
2. Reduction in bisecting glycans due to a reduced expression of MGAT3 (GnT-III);
3. Increased branching due to high MGAT5 (GnT-V) expression, which facilitates formation of complex glycans,
4. Increased fucosylation of the innermost GlcNAc residue (core fucosylation) and 5. Terminal modifications like sialylation, fucosylation, lactose addition etc. (Fig. 2). These modifications also allow formation of selectin-binding structures like sLeX or sLeA, promoting extravasation of circulating tumour cells. Formation of bisecting glycans and N-glycan branching often display opposite effects on metastasis. Studies on the OvCa cell line SKOV3 and its highly metastatic derivative, SKOV3-ip, have shown up-regulation of high-mannose and complex glycans, whereas bisecting glycans were down-regulated in metastatic cells[41]. By mass spectrometry or lectin staining, increased levels of N-glycan branching with tri- and tetraantennary

structures and sialylation have been detected in highly metastatic prostate cancer cell lines[42]. Breast cancer cells are characterized by dramatic increases in high-mannose and complex tri-antennary N-glycans compared to normal tissue[43]. In our own analysis of a breast cancer cohort, positive binding results for Galanthus nivalis lectin (GNA; detecting high-mannose structures) and Phaseolus vulgaris leucoagglutinin (PHA-L; detecting complex N-glycans with terminal Gal, GalNAc and Man) correlated with vascular invasion and, partly, lymph node involvement[8]. In another histochemical study, increased PHA-L binding in breast cancer metastases compared to primary tumours and a shorter survival in PHA-l-positive patients was found, suggesting that complex 1,6-branched N-glycans promote breast cancer progression[44]. Yet, glycan changes during tumourigenesis partly vary in different tumour entities. In example, complex N-glycans were rarely found in ovarian carcinoma tissue[45] and imaging MS techniques showed that OvCa cells predominantly expressed high-mannose N-glycans whereas complex glycans were mainly detected in the tumour stroma[46]. Similarly, bisecting N-glycans and terminal GalNAc-GlcNAc (lacdiNAc) structures are elevated in OvCa cells and tissue, but low in breast cancer[47]. Sialylation is a feature of many complex glycans. In various cancer types, an increased sialylation of N-glycans has been shown which contributes to the stability and activity of target proteins (reviewed by[48]). In hepatocarcinoma cells, sialylated N-glycans promoted cell invasionand adhesionto lymphnodes as well as lymphatic metastasis in vivo, and neuraminidase treatment reverted this effect[40]. A specific modifification is addition of poly Nacetyllactosamine (polylacNAc) to complex N-glycans. PolylacNAc is a high-affifinity ligand for galectin-3, which is expressed constitutively in the lung including vascular epithelia, and has been reported to facilitate lung metastasis in melanoma[49]. Inhibition of the galectin-3/PolylacNAc interactionblocks cancer cell adhesion and experimental metastasis[50].

Enzymes involved in N-glycosylation and metastasis: Several glycosylation enzymes have been shown to be associated with metastasis in experimental studies or clinical tumour tissues, without further knowledge aboutthe targetproteins, which are responsible for these effects: RPN1 (ribophorin), as part of the OST complex, has been shown to facilitate N-glycosylation of specirific substrates, while it is not involved in modifification of other molecules[65]. Interestingly, high RPN1 mRNA levels in two breast cancer cohorts were significantly associated with shorter recurrence-free survival, even in multivariate analysis, and high RPN1 expression was associated with the presence of distantmetastasis[36]. RPN2 expressionas determined by IHC has also been reported to be associated with aggressive features of breast cancer, and the combination ofRPN2 and p53 positivity correlated with poor prognosis[66].

Aprognostic impact was shown in human osteosarcoma patients, where high RPN2 expression correlates with a high frequency of metastasis after initial diagnosis, In a xenograft model using highly metastatic osteosarcoma cells, RPN2 silencing led to a reduced tumour growth and lung metastasis[67] and in colorectal carcinomas, high RPN2 mRNA or protein levels correlated with distant metastasis[68]. N33 (TUSC3) also associates with the OST complex where it regulates N-glycosylation of specirific substrates. It was suggested as a potential tumour suppressor in various tumour types including prostate carcinoma, pancreatic cancer or head and neck squamous cell carcinomas[69]. In the latter tumour, loss of N33 correlated with advanced stage, lymph node involvement and poor survival. Pils et al. detected TUSC3 methylation in ovarian cancer samples, where it correlated with signifificantly shorter RFS and OAS. Reconstitution of N33 expression in two ovarian and pancreatic cell lines decreased adhesion to collagen[70] suggesting a role of Nglycosylation in ovarian cancer progression, and TUSC3 silencingin OvCa cell lines enhanced migration and proliferation[71].

In addition to RPN1, our own microarray study revealed additional N-glycosylation enzymes with prognostic relevance in breast cancer: The trimming enzymes GCS1 and GANAB were associated with shorter survival and distant metastasis, whereas high levels of the Golgi mannosidase MAN1A1 which degrades high-mannose glycans correlated with favorable prognosis in this tumour type[36]. MAN1A1 was also found to be down-regulated in metastatic hepatocellular cancer (HCC) cell lines and orthotopic xenograft tumours as compared to non-metastatic HCC controls in a small study on transcriptional profifiling of glycogenes[22]. MGAT5 overexpression in cancer cells generally leads to an increase in 1-6 GlcNAc branching, which is necessary for formation of complex tri- and tetraantennary structures associated with the metastatic phenotype[72]. Accordingly, in immunohistochemical studies MGAT5 was associated with metastasis and poor prognosis in hepatocellular and renal carcinomas[73,74]. ST6GAL1 which catalyzes transfer of sialic acids to terminal galactose residues of N-glycans is up-regulated in numerous cancers where it is associated with changes in adhesion, migration, invasion, and poor prognosis for patients. ST6GAL1 up-regulation led to metastatic spread in human CRC cells[75].

Similarly, high ST6GAL1 levels in mammary carcinoma cells and human anaplastic large cell lymphoma led to increased adhesion to ECM structures and increased invasiveness[76]. FUT8 catalyzes fucosylation of the innermost GlcNAc residue of N-glycans (core fucosylation). In several experimental studies, high FUT8 expression in cancer cells leads to higher motility and metastatic potential, and in breast cancer or NSCLC, it was associated with signifificantly shorter OAS and RFS[77,78]. Interestingly, core fucosylation of E-cadherin leads to higher adhesion and less migration in experimental systems[79,80]. Thus, the prognostic impact of FUT8 cannot depend on this adhesion molecule. In gastric cancer which is frequently linked to E-cadherin loss, there are less core-fucosylated structures and FUT8 is downregulated in cancer cells[81].

18. Target proteins of N-glycosylation involved in metastasis

Glycosylation of adhesion proteins can largely influence their binding properties, leading to altered cell-cell or cell-matrix contacts and contributing to EMT. N-glycosylation of **E-cadherin** has strong impact on its function as adhesion molecule, signalling protein and tumour-suppressor. Promoter analyses have shown that expression of the fifirst enzyme of N-glycosylation, DPAG1, is activated by the Wnt/-catenin pathway which results in strong N-glycosylation of E-cadherin and reduction of cell-cell adhesion in adherens junctions[51]. In normal epithelial cells, E-cadherin has been shown to harbor mainly bisecting N-glycans due to the activity of the MGAT3 enzyme. In carcinoma cells, MGAT3 is frequently down-regulated by promoter methylation and its counterpart MGAT5 is up-regulated leading to the formation of tri- and tetraantennary complex glycans on cadherins and other proteins. This results in E-cadherin internalization to the cytoplasm and disruption of cell-cell contacts, which compromises the associated signalling pathways, resulting in EMT, invasion and metastasis[52].

Further analysis revealed that especially the formation of complex branched glycans at Asn-554 of E-cadherin leads to disruption of E-cadherin dimers and promotes tumourigenesis in gastric cancer cells[53]. The antagonist of E-cadherin in EMT, N-Cadherin, also contains N-glycosylation sites which are relevant for homophilic adhesion: Knockdown of MGAT5 expression in fifibrosarcoma cells resulted in decreased levels of complex glycans, increased cell-cell contacts, decreased migration and invasion as well as enhanced outside-in signalling as shown by ERK phosphorylation [54]. N-glycosylation has also been shown to be essential for **integrins** and their role in metastasis. Integrin 64 is dependent on N-glycosylation of the 4 subunit for proper cell adhesion, migration on laminin and signalling[55].

Overexpression of MGAT5 in HT1080 fibrosarcoma cells resulted in decreased adhesion to fifibronectin, but increased migration and invasion, caused by enhanced N-glycan branching of 1-integrin[56]. MGAT5 expression is stimulated by several oncogenes like src, HER2/neu, ras etc., whose activity can be partly explained by their effects on N-glycosylation. The activity of integrins is partly regulated by sialylation oftheir N-glycans. In colorectal cancer cells, overexpression of ST6GAL1 lead to highly sialylated integrin 1, increased adhesion to collagen I and laminin and enhanced migration[57]. Conversely, up-regulation of the neuraminidase neu1 induced desialylationof 4 integrin and reduced liver metastases inamouse model[58]. Experiments with overexpression of either MGAT3 or MGAT5 in gastric cancer cells demonstrated thatthe integrin ligand laminin-332 is also N-glycosylated, and that increased N-glycan branching has an inflfluence on integrin clustering, cell motility and adhesion[59]. CD44 isoforms are highly O- and N-glycosylated adhesion proteins. Sialic-acid capped N-glycans of CD44 inhibit its binding to hyaluronan which has strong impact on cell migration[60].

Cancer cell invasion depends on the activity of proteolytic enzymes, which cooperate to degrade the extracellular matrix. Matrix-metalloproteinases (MMPs) degrade a variety of substrates, and their expression is partly associated with an unfavorable prognosis in various tumour types. Several MMPs harbor N-glycosylation sites within their catalytic domain, but their functional meaning is only poorly understood (summarized by[61]). In HT1080 leukemia cells, MMP1 carries highly complex glycans, which frequently end in sialyl Lewis X antigens. Thus, MMP1 might bind to the surface of activated, selectin-presenting endothelial cells, promoting invasion and metastasis. The MMP9 N-glycans are partially sialylated, core-fucosylated structures, and sialidase treatment alters interaction with the MMP inhibitor TIMP1[61].

N-glycosylation has also been reported for kallikreins[62] and cathepsins. For cathepsin V, proper N-glycosylation is required for secretion and enzyme activity in human tumour cells[63]. Similar to O-glycans, N-glycans can inflfluence the process of adhesion to endothelial cells and extravasation since complex Nglycans might harbor selectin-binding sites like sLeX. In CRISP/Cas experiments blocking either O-glycosylation, N-glycosylation or synthesis of glycolipids in leukemia cells, N-glycans were important for E-selectin binding and rolling on endothelial cells, while O-glycans were essentialfor P- and L-selectin interactions[64]. Glycosylated CD44v isoforms also confer E-selectin binding of breast cancer cells under physiological shear conditions. Surprisingly, experiments with selective inhibitors of O- or N-glycosylation demonstrated that the responsible CD44 epitopes are presented by N-glycans[21].

19. Glycosaminoglycans (GAGs)

Biosynthesis and types of GAGs:GAGs are long unbranched polysaccharides consisting of repeating disaccharide units, one of the sugars being either Nacetylglucosamine (GlcNAc) or N-acetylgalactosamine (GalNAc) and the other being an uronic acid (glucuronic acid or iduronic acid) or galactose. GAGs can be classifified into six major categories: hyaluronan (HA), chondroitin sulfate (CS) and dermatan sulfate (DS), heparin and heparan sulfate (HS) and keratan sulfate (Fig. 3A). The GAG polysaccharide backbones, excepting hyaluronan, can be modifified by sulfatation and uronate epimerization, leading to a substantial degree of structural variability that in turn accounts for a wide diversity of biological activities. Sulfated GAG chains are synthetized in the Golgi apparatus by extending a preformed tetrasacharide (GlcUA-Gal-Gal-Xyl-), which is attached to a serine residue of the backbone protein, with disaccharide repeats. Subsequently, GAG chains are modifified by sulfation at various positions and epimerization at GlcUA residues. A variety of enzymes including glycosyltransferases, sulfatases and epimerase are involved in this process[82].

Synthesis of CS, DS, heparin and heparan sulfate is initiated by the attachment of xylose to specifific serine residues. This process, known as xylosylation, depends on UDP-xylose levels and on the activity of xylosyltransferases and regulates the number and location of the GAG chains. In contrast to the rest of GAGs, HA lacks a covalent bond to protein structures, but instead can interact non-covalently with proteoglycans via hyaluronan-binding motifs. HA is synthesized on the inner cell surface by hyaluronan synthases (HAS1, HAS2 and HAS3) and simultaneously extrudedto the outside ofthe cell, where it is either released into the ECM, remains attached to the plasma membrane or is internalized again. Degradation of HA requires hyaluronidases (HYAL1 and HYAL2). Here, the concerted action of certain hyaluronan synthases and hyaluronidases leads to the formation of different HA-size fragments that have wide-ranging and often opposing functions.

Which proteins carry GAG chains?

Proteoglycans (PG) comprise a protein backbone to which one or more GAG chains are covalently attached. Although most proteoglycans also contain O- and N-glycans, the GAG chains are much larger and dominate the chemical and functional characteristics of this class of glycoproteins. Depending on their localization, proteoglycans can be grouped into three categories: extracellular, membrane-bound and intracellular proteoglycans (Fig. 3B).

- Serglycin is the only proteoglycan present in the **cytoplasm**, where it is packaged in storage granules. In connective tissue mast cells, serglycin carries several heparin chains and therefore represents a unique proteoglycan containing this GAG type[83].

- Diverse**membrane-associated**proteoglycans are known, mainly carrying CS (syndecan-1/-3, NG2 and betaglycan) and/or HS chains (syndecan-2/-4, betaglycan, and glypican). Syndecans consist of an intracellular domain, transmembrane and ectodomain, which allow interactions with a variety of extracellular ligands (i.e. growth factors and ECM components) leading to signal transduction events[84]. NG2 (neuron glia antigen-2) and betaglycan TGFtype III receptor) are transmembrane proteoglycans carrying CS and HS/CS, respectively. Further transmembrane proteoglycans are phosphacan, which is mainly expressed in the CNS and carries KS or CS chains, and certain splice forms of CD44 (CD44v3) that carry HS and/or CS and can bind hyaluronan. In contrast, glypicans are bound to the plasma membrane via a GPI anchor and carry only HS chains.

A large diversity of proteoglycans is present within the **ECM**. Among them, the biggest family is the small leucine-rich proteoglycan (SLRPs) group, consisting of at least 20 members, i.e. biglycan, decorin, lumican, which carry CS, DS, or KS chains. Further, the aggrecan family of proteoglycans that includes aggrecan, versican, brevican, and neurocan, mainly carrying CS, has been shown to contain additional hyaluronan binding domains. The basement membrane separates epithelial cells from the underlying lamina propia and consists mainly oflaminin, proteoglycans and collagens, which can also carry GAG chains. Among the proteoglycans, perlecan, agrin, collagen XV (all carrying HS) and collagen type XVIII (carrying CS) are the best characterized.

GAGs/Proteoglycans and metastasis

Within the glycosaminoglycan family only heparan sulphate, chondroitin/dermatan sulphate and hyaluronan show a welldocumented role in cancer progression.

Chondroitin sulfate (CS) is composed of repeating disaccharides of GalNAc and D-glucuronic acid (GlcA) with different sulfation patterns, mediated by specifific carbohydrate sulfotransferases (CHSTs): CS-A [GlcA-GalNAc-4-sulfate] and CS-C [GlcA-GalNAc-6-O-sulfate] contain monosulfated units, whereas CS-D [GlcA(2-O-sulfate)–GalNAc(6-O-sulfate)] and CS-E show multiple sulfation patterns[85]. The sulfation of CS strongly influences the biological function of these GAG and represent a critical factor in cancer progression[86].

A variable effect of CS/CSPGs (chondroitin sulfate proteoglycans) has been described depending on their localization. Tumour cell-associated CS/CSPGs seem to promote migration and invasion. Here, oncofetal CS chains (ofCS), which are normally restricted to the placenta, have been found in proteoglycans of tumour and tumour-infiltrated stromal cells in several cancer entities and blocking of these structures led toreduced migration, invasion and anchorage-independent growth in vitro as well as inhibited seeding and spreading of tumour cells in vivo[87]. Also, in invasive brain tumours several CSPG core proteins have been described to promote tumour cell invasion[88–90].

In 2001, Iida et al. described the key role of CS in the MMPmediated human melanoma invasion. The same group could later show that chondroitin 4-sulfate (C4S) but not chondroitin 6-sulfate (C6S) binds and facilitates activation of pro-MMP2, strongly affecting tumour cell invasion[91,92]. In contrast, other studies showed that CSPGs localized in the ECM strongly inhibit tumour cell invasion of human glioma cells[93]. In line with these data, decorin and chondroitin-6-sulfate inhibit B16V melanoma cell migration and invasion by acidifification of the cellular suface[94]. On the contrary, and increasing the complexity of CS function in metastasis, small CS-E fragments, present in the ECM, enhance tumour cell motility via inducing CD44 shedding[95]. Tumour cell interactions with platelets and endothelial cells are of key importance for extravasation and subsequent colonization. CSPGs present on the surface of highly metastatic cancer cells mediate this essential adhesion step via binding to P-selectin, which is highly expressed on activated platelets and endothelial cells[96].

Here, the CS sulfation pattern seems to play an important role, since only CS-E and CS-B, but not CS-C/D, bind to P- and to some extent to L-selectin [97]. Further, CS-A has been described to regulate fifibrosarcoma cell adhesion and migration via JNK and tyrosine kinase signalling pathways [98].Another important aspect of CS function is the interaction with growth factors in the ECM. Thus, CS chains bind and store growth factors being able to release them progressively. In example, FGF2 can be bound by CS-E and CS-A building a complex with the corresponding receptor and thereby regulating its activation[99].

Heparan sulfate (HS) is composed of alternate units of GlcNAc and uronic acid with the GlcNAc residues often being further processed by acetyl group removal and subsequent sulfatation. HS is located at the cell surface and within the ECM −as HSPG (heparan sulfate proteoglycan)- and modulates cell-cell and cell-ECM interactions. The role of diverse HSPGs (i.e. syndecans, glypicans and perlecan) on metastasis has been exhaustively analysed in the past years, whereas less information exists about the direct function of HS chains in this process. Originally, HS was considered as anti-tumourigenic, since reduced levels of HS chains correlated with high metastatic activity in different tumour entities, in part due toreduced cell-cell adhesion and increased invasion[100].

Recently, it has been recognized that the same HSPG might act as either inhibitor or promoter of tumour cell progression depending not only on the cancer type and stage but also on the modulation of the HS chains. A direct implication of the HS chains in syndecan- 1function has been demonstrated by analyzing the bioactivity of different syndecan-1 forms bearing mutations in one or more HS binding sites. As the number of HS chains attached to syndecan- 1 decreased, its ability to inhibit invasion was also reduced[101]. Similarly, blocking of HS chains in glypican-3 with a specific antibody inhibits migration of hepatocellular carcinoma cells[102].

Hyaluronan is composed of disaccharide repeats of GlcUA and GlcNAc bound alternately by -1,3 and -1,4 glycosidic bonds. As described above, these polymers are hydrolysed by hyaluronidases, thereby leading to a big variety of HA chain lengths. Thus, the sizes and quantity of the HA polymers and the expression of HA-associated enzymes impact tumour progression in a manifold manner. Newly synthetized HA is located pericellularly, mainly attached to specifific receptors, or in the ECM modulating the cell microenviroment. In addition, HA fragments may interact with their receptors, i.e. CD44, RHAMM,

LYVE-1, acting as a signal mediator of key importance during tumour progression. By attaching to CD44, newly synthesized HA chains provide a highly hydrated environment that facilitates migration and invasion of breast cancer cells[103]. Recently, several studies described low molecular weight hyaluronan (LMW-HA) as a key player for tumour progression and metastasis. LMW-HA induces cell motility via upregulationof MMPs, invasionas well as integrin-mediated adhesion to endothelial cells[104,105].

20. Proteoglycans involved in metastasis

The structural and functional diversity as well as their abundance and location predestine proteoglycans as key molecules in the metastatic cascade. Indeed, depending on the PG type, tumour entity and structure of the GAG chains, PGs have been described to either promote or inhibit carcinogenesis.

Syndecan-1 loss is associated with EMT and accelerated tumour progression in some cancer types[106], whereas in others like myeloma or breast cancer it shows an anti-tumourigenic function, namely it raises cell-matrix adhesion and inhibits invasion. Here, a direct implication of the HS chains has been demonstrated by analyzing different syndecan-1 forms bearingmutations inone ormore HS binding sites. As the number of HS chains attached to syndecan- 1 decreases, the ability to inhibit invasion was also reduced[101]. Controversial functions have also been described for syndecan- 4 in melanoma cells: While one study reports increased motility and decreased attachment on fibronectin[107], a different study shows reduced invasionafter syndecan-4 knock downby decreased Wnt5A signalling[108]. The role of glypican family members in carcinogenesis also varies depending on the cell of origin.

Glypican-3 is down-regulated in some human tumours, including mesothelioma, breast and ovariancancer. In breast cancer cells decreased glypican-3 expression lead to reduced adhesion to fibronectin and increased migration in vitro as well as metastasis in vivo. In contrast, GPC3 overexpression is associated with a poor prognosis for patients with HCC, and it may also have predictive potentialfor HCC invasion and metastasis[109]. A reduced expression of Glypican-5 in non-small lung cancer samples has been described compared to adjacent noncancerous tissues. Here, overexpression of glypican-5 in NSCLC cell lines signifificantly reduced their migration and invasion[110]. Further, both glypican-3 and glypican-5 suppress EMT in breast cancer and lung adenocarcinoma, respectively[111].

Serglycin is mainly found in secretory granules or vesicles in cells of hematopoietic origin, where it modulates the secretion of proteases, chemokines, or other cytokines. In breast and nasopharyngeal cancer, secreted serglycin has been found to promote metastasis via increasing the migratory and invasive properties of tumour cells[112,113]. Perlecan, the most abundant HSPG of epithelial and endothelial basement membranes, has been shown to promote cell invasion[114]. Its down-regulation inhibits tumour growth and angiogenesis in vivo and suppresses the invasive behavior of melanoma cells in vitro[115,116]. Biglycan, a SLRP family member, is secreted by tumour-associated endothelial cells and activates tumour cell migration thereby promoting metastatis[117,118]. Versican regulates the development of peritoneal metastasis in ovarian cancer by promoting adhesion of tumour cells and tumour cell spheroids tomesothelial cells as well as subsequent spheroid disaggregation[119].

21. GAG-related enzymes involved in metastasis

In addition to the GAG structures themselves diverse **enzymes** involved in their synthesis and/or modulation play an important role for metastatic spread of tumour cells. Chondroitin sulfotransferase 11 (**CHST11**) has been described to be relevant for ovarian cancer progression and to play a key role in breast cancer metastasis via regulation of P-selectin ligands[85,120]. The evidence that diverse heparan sulfate-proteases strongly inflfluence metastasis supports indirectly the pivotal role of the HS chains themselves during this process. Interestingly, a recent study has shown that after HS chain cleavage HSPG core proteins may undergo new bindings thereby initiating downstream pro-tumourigenic signalling events[121]. The catabolic enzyme **heparanase**, that cleaves intact HS chains in basement membranes, the underlying ECM and on the cell surface, has been repeatedly described as a potent tumour promotor[122,123]. Main consequences of heparanase activity are the release of growth factors and cytokines, i.e. angiogenic factors, and remodeling of the extracellular matrix.

Thus, the heparanase-mediated disassembly of the tumour cell environment promotes invasion and metastasis. Syndecan-1 and perlecan are targets of heparanase, and their degradation modulates tumour cell invasion and metastasis[124]. Furthermore, heparanase expression increases cell adhesion by cleavage of HS chains of syndecans and glypicans[125–127] in various cell types reviewed by Levy-Adam et al.[128]. Also the expression of HA-related enzymes has been reported to influence metastasis by not fully clarified mechanisms[129]. Hyaluronan synthase 2 (**HAS2**) promotes tumour cell invasion via deregulation of TIMP-1, and **HAS3** (hyaluronan synthase 3) inhibition led to a decreased pericellular HA matrix thereby inhibiting anchorage-independent growth in primary colon carcinoma cells[130].

In contrast, increased expression of HAS2 and HAS3 promotes tumour cell adhesion to bone marrow endothelial cells, presumably via increasing the cell surface hyaluronan matrix [131]. Unexpectedly, hyaluronidases also correlate with tumour progression: **HYAL1** promotes tumour cell proliferation, motility and invasion[132–134], and increased levels of LMW-HA, which has been previously described as pro-metastatic, are associated with overexpression of HAS2 as well as HYAL1 and HYAL2[105].

Several enzymes involved in the synthesis and modulation ofGAG correlate signifificantly with distant metastasis, and interestingly some of them with metastasis to specifific organ sites in breast cancer. Here, high HAS2 and HYAL1 mRNA levels were associated with brain metastasis, whereas tumours metastasizing to the lung and bone showed increased expression of CSGALNACT2 (chondroitin sulfate N-acetylgalactosaminyltransferase) and XYLT2 (xylosyltransferase 2), respectively[36]

22. Novel Prognosticators of OSCC

We investigated the hallmarks of cancer-related molecules to elucidate the molecular mechanism of cancer development, invasion, metastasis, and prognosis. Here, we describe the functions of 12 new prognostic factors in OSCC (Table 1).

2.1. miR-126

MicroRNAs (miRNAs) are noncoding small RNAs of approximately 18–25 nucleotides that regulate gene expression by binding to the *30*-untranslated region (UTR) of the target mRNA[6]. The biosynthetic process of the mature miRNA can be explained as follows. Primary miRNA (pri-miRNA) is processed in the nucleus into precursor miRNA (pre-miRNA) by the RNase Drosha and DiGeorge syndrome critical region gene 8 (*DCRG8*). Pre-miRNA is exported to the cytoplasm by exportin-5 and processed into mature miRNA by the RNase Dicer. After integration into the RNA-induced silencing complex (RISC), the mature miRNA regulates the target gene mRNA expression[6].

Recently, meta-analyses have revealed that the upregulation of 9 miRNAs (*miR-21*, *miR-455-5p*, *miR-155-5p*, *miR-372*, *miR-373*, *miR-29b*, *miR-1246*, *miR-196a*, and *miR-181*) and the downregulation of 7 miRNAs (*miR-204*, *miR-101*, *miR-32*, *miR-20a*, *miR-16*, *miR-17*, and *miR-125b*) are strongly correlated with poor prognosis in OSCC patients[83]. Long noncoding RNA (lncRNA), a class of non-protein coding transcripts longer than 200 nucleotides, is also associated with gene expression and cancer progression[84]. Among them, HOX transcript antisense RNA (*HOTAIR*)[84], metastasis-associated lung adenocarcinoma transcript 1 (*MALAT1*)[85] and *lncRNA H1*[86] are predictors of poor survival in OSCC. *miR-126* is an endothelial, cell-specifific miRNA located in intron 7 of epidermal growth factor-like domain 7 (*EGFL7*) and its overexpression promotes vessel formation by repressing expression of sprouty-related protein-1 (Spred-1) in developmental angiogenesis[6,87]. Previously, we reportedthat miR-126 and its host gene, *EGFL7*, were downregulated by DNA hypermethylation in OSCC cells[88]. In addition, *miR-126* is a negative regulator of VEGF-A activation and promotes tumor cell growth in OSCC cells. In human OSCC specimens, a low *miR-126* expression was observed in 94 of 118 cases (79.7%) and was relevant to local tumor expansion (T grade), clinical stage, and nodal metastasis. Besides, the reduced *miR-126* expression correlated with tumor angiogenesis and lymphangiogenesis and poorer outcomes. Furthermore, multivariate analysis revealed that *miR-126* expression levels were independent prognostic factors for disease-free survival periods in OSCC.

TANGO	Upregulated	Sustaining proliferative signaling Activating invasion and metastasis Inducing angiogenesis Resisting cell death
ME1	Upregulated	Sustaining proliferative signaling Activating invasion and metastasis Deregulating energetics
miR-126	Downregulated	Sustaining proliferative signaling Evading growth suppressors Inducing angiogenesis
FOXC2	Upregulated	Inducing angiogenesis
PROX1	Upregulated	Sustaining proliferative signaling Activating invasion and metastasis Inducing angiogenesis
HuD	Upregulated	Activating invasion and metastasis Resisting cell death
STOX2	Upregulated	Sustaining proliferative signaling Avoiding immune destruction Activating invasion and metastasis Resisting cell death
PAUF	Upregulated	Sustaining proliferative signaling[95] Activating invasion and metastasis Inducing angiogenesis Resisting cell death
ME1	upregulated	Sustaining proliferative signaling[58] activating invasion and metastasis deregulating energetics

TANGO: transport and Golgi organization protein 1; ME1: malic enzyme 1; FOXC2: forkhead box protein C2; PROX1: prospero homeobox 1; HuD: Hu antigen D; STOX2: Storkhead box protein 2; N4BP2L1: NEDD4-binding protein 2-like 1; ZFAND4: zinc fifinger AN1-type containing 4; NIPL1: NIPA-like domain containing 1; LEMD1: LEM domain containing 1; PAUF: pancreatic adenocarcinoma upregulated factor.

2.2. FOXC2

Forkhead box protein C2 (FOXC2) is a transcriptional regulatory factor which is essential to cardiovascular development, including vascular endothelial cell differentiation and lymphatic vesselformation [96]. Reportedly, FOXC2 is a tumor-progressive factor in various malignancies and is closely associated with metastasis and prognosis[97–99]. In addition, FOXC2 regulated EMT and the gain of multiple anticancer drug resistance in cancer cells[89,100]. In OSCC, immunostaining for FOXC2 was observed in 23.3% (38/163) of cases and markedly related to MVD[101]. In addition, cases with FOXC2-positive OSCC exhibited markedly poorer prognosis than those with FOXC2-negative OSCC. In the functional analysis under a coculture of human OSCC cells and vascularendothelial cells, FOXC2 promoted angiogenesis by enhancing VEGF-A expression. Furthermore, FOXC2 regulated the gene expression of prospero homeobox 1 (PROX1) in OSCC cells. Our results suggested that FOXC2 could be a novel angiogenic inducer in OSCC cells.

2.3. PROX1

PROX1 is a nuclear transcription factor associated with the embryonic development of multiple organs, including the central nervous system, heart, lymphatic system, skeletal muscles, lens, retina, and so on[102]. Reportedly, PROX1 plays various tumor-dependent functional roles, which reflect both the oncogenic potential and a tumor-suppressive role[90]. In addition, PROX1 promoted cell growth, angiogenesis, and sorafenib resistance in patients with

HCC[91,102] and is associated with the lymphangiogenesis, metastasis, and poor prognosis in various malignancies[92,103,104]. However, high PROX1 expression is related to better prognosis for pancreatic and gastric cancer patients[105,106].

Thus, PROX1's role in malignancies remains debatable. The PROX1 expression was found in 25.8% (42/163) of patients with OSCC by immunohistochemistry and was markedly associated with the local progression of the tumor (T classification), clinical stage, LVD, nodal metastasis, and expression levels of FOXC2[101]. Besides, the survival and multivariate analysis revealed that PROX1 expressioncorrelated with poor survival of OSCC patients. PROX1 also accelerated cell growth and lymphangiogeneis through VEGF-C activation in OSCC cells. Our findings indicated that PROX1 exhibits tumor-progressive function in OSCC. However, reportedly, the PROX1 reduction promoted OSCC cell proliferation[107]. Hence, further studies are warranted to elucidate the detailed molecular mechanisms underlying PROX1 in OSCC.

2.4. TANGO

Reportedly, *MIA* and *MIA2* are involved in OSCC tumor progression[27,52]. The expression of the *MIA* gene family members is reported in several malignancies[93]. Transport and Golgi organization protein 1 (*TANGO*) is one of the *MIA* gene family members and comprises a highly conserved Src homology 3 (SH3)-like domain[4]. *TANGO* could be a suppressor of the invasion and migration of malignant melanoma, colorectal cancer (CRC) and HCC[108,109]. However, the *TANGO* expression reportedly correlated with tumor progression, nodal and distant metastasis, and shortened disease-free survival in SCC of the esophagus, lung, and uterine cervix[93]. In OSCC, *TANGO* also regulated adhesion to OSCC cells, transendothelial migration, and tube formation of vascular and lymphatic vascular endothelial cells by activating the platelet-derived growth factor-β polypeptide (PDGFB) and neuropilin 2[4,54].

Imatinib, an inhibitor of the PDGF receptor tyrosine kinase, might be useful for OSCC treatment because of decreased *TANGO* activity[4]. In addition, *TANGO* promoted migration and invasion while inhibiting apoptosis in human OSCC cells. We observed the *TANGO* expression in 35.1% (60/171) of OSCC specimens, markedly correlating with age, tumor progression (T grade) clinical stage, nodal metastasis, MVD and LVD. Moreover, survival analysis elucidated markedly shorter disease-free survival periods in patients with the *TANGO* expression than in those without the *TANGO* expression. As the *MIA* gene family members are also secretory proteins[110], *TANGO* might be useful as a tumor marker detectable in the serum, saliva, urine, ascites and pleural fluid, and other samples[4,93]. Our fifindings suggested that *TANGO* exhibits tumor-progressive function in its activation of angiogenesis and lymphangiogenesis in OSCC

2.5. HuD

Hu antigen D (HuD) serves as an RNA-binding protein involved in mRNA stability and translational modulation. It contains an Au-rich element present in 30 -UTR and neuronal differentiation[94]. The leading target mRNAs of HuD are growth-associated protein 43 (GAP43), acetylcholine transferase (AchE), p21, c-myc, N-myc, Notch3, VEGF-A, and so on[111]. Previously, HuD expression has been reported in small cell lung carcinoma and neuroblastoma[112,113]. In addition, we previously reported that HuD regulated the invasion ability and activation of caspase-3, and the main target genes in OSCC cells of HuD are *VEGF-A, VEGF-D, MMP-2,* and *MMP-9*[114]. In OSCC specimens, HuD expression was detected in 36.6% (30/82), and its expression closely correlated with the histological differentiation of the tumor, nodal metastasis, and diffuse invasion pattern. Moreover, a survival curve analysis revealed markedly worse outcomes in patients with the HuD expression than patients who were HuD-negative, and the HuD expression was an independent prognostic predictor in patients with OSCC. Besides, HuD is a useful diagnostic and therapeutic target in OSCC. As MMP-2 and -9 are components of the epithelial basement membrane and extracellular matrix proteins, HuD could be a novel modulator for the tumor microenvironmental modification in OSCC[114]. Furthermore, our results suggested that HuD is newly detected target of VEGF-A–mediated angiogenesis in OSCC.

2.6. *STOX2*

Storkhead box protein 2 (STOX2) is considered a transcriptional factor, and its expression is decreased in the decidual tissue of patients with fetal growth restriction[115]. A prior cDNA microarray analysis revealed that *STOX2* expression is related to prognosis in CRC[116]. Conversely, a study reported that *STOX2* expression levels in CRC were decreased by CpG island hypermethylation of the *STOX2* promoter region[95]. Hence, the role of STOX2 in malignancies remains unclear. In OSCC cells, STOX2 expression levels were increased by *MIA*, secretory protein of melanoma, in a paracrine manner[117]. In addition, STOX2 modulated the cell growth, invasion, and inhibition of apoptosis in OSCC cells by interacting with *MIA*. Moreover, STOX2 promoted resistance to paclitaxel, cisplatin, and 5-FU in OSCC. In fact, immunostaining of STOX2 was observed in 28.7% (58/202) of OSCC cases and associated with nodal metastasis, *MIA* expression, and poor survival. Multivariate analysis revealed that STOX2 expression was an independent predictor of disease-free survival in OSCC patients. Interestingly, STOX2 expression was also observed in the stromal plasma cells surrounding OSCC. Although further studies are warranted to validate STOX2's role in the tumor stroma, it might contribute to the disruption of the host immune system. Hence, the *MIA*–STOX2 pathway might be a useful molecular target in OSCC.

2.7. N4BP2L1

Previously, we compared the gene expression profiles of primary and recurrent OSCC using cDNA microarray analysis, and the most increased level of expression in recurrent OSCC was NEDD4-binding protein 2-like 1 (*N4BP2L1*)[118]. Although N4BP2L1 is a critical paralog of N4BP2, highly expressed in nasopharyngeal carcinoma[119], little information was available about the functional role of N4BP2L1 in tumor cells. We determined that N4BP2L1 enhances invasion ability and miR-448 inversely regulates N4BP2L1 expression in OSCC cells[118]. In addition, the N4BP2L1 expression was observed in 34.8% (65/187) of OSCC cases by immunohistochemistry, and a marked correlation was observed between the N4BP2L1 expression and nodal metastasis. A gene expression analysis of 45 OSCC samples indicated lower *miR-448* expression levels were conversely associated with *N4BP2L1* upregulation. Moreover, the N4BP2L1 overexpression correlated with poor outcome and was an independent predictor of disease-free survival in OSCC patients. Hence, N4BP2L1 could be a new target for diagnosis and treatment of OSCC.

2.8. ZFAND4

Zinc finger AN1-type containing 4 (*ZFAND4*) is one of the most upregulated genes in recurrent OSCC samples [118]. Although higher *ZFAND4* expression, regulated by miR-182, strongly correlated with clinical stage progression in gastric cancer [120], little information is available about the functional roles of ZFAND4 in malignancies. Accordingly, we assessed the immunostaining of ZFAND4 in 214 OSCC cases[121]. The cytoplasmic expression of ZFAND4 was detected in 21% (45/214) of OSCC cases, and there appears to be a link between ZFAND4 expression and lymph node metastasis, lymphatic invasion, vascular infifiltration, and poorer outcome. In addition, the ZFAND4 overexpression was considered an independent predictor of unfavorable prognosis in OSCC cases as revealed by a multivariate analysis. Intriguingly, high ZFAND4 expression was also implicated in distant OSCC metastasis. While 3.8–12.6% OSCC patients experience metastasis, the disease becomes highly lethal when metastasis occurs[121,122]. Hence, ZFAND4 could be an essential molecular marker and therapeutic target for distant metastasis and prognosis of OSCC cells.

2.9. NIPAL1

Previously, we identifified NIPA-like domain containing 1 (*NIPAL1*) as an overexpressed gene in recurrent OSCC[118]. *NIPAL1* is a membranous magnesium transporter and has been associated with the pathogenesis of gout and hyperuricemia by indirect urate transport regulation[123]. Research has demonstrated that hyperuricemia is associated with an increased risk of cancer[124]. However, little is known about the *NIPAL1*'s role in malignancies. In OSCC cells, *NIPAL1* accelerated cancer cell proliferation and adhesion to vascular endothelial cells (intravasation)[125]. However, *NIPAL1* failed to affect the transendothelial migration, tube formation, and branching of endothelial cells. Perhaps *NIPAL1* might merely accelerate OSCC cell infifiltration that had been evoked by other angiogenic factors. The *NIPAL1* expression was detected in 20.3% (39/192) of OSCC cases and correlated strongly with vascular invasion and short disease-free survival. Furthermore, the *NIPAL1* expression was an independent predictor of poor prognosis in OSCC patients.

2.10. LEMD1

LEM domain containing 1 (*LEMD1*) comprises several splicing variants, and LEMD1 variant 1 (V1), V2, and V3 are cancer-testis antigens (CTA)[126]. Reportedly, LEMD1 overexpression has been detected in colon cancer, prostate cancer, and anaplastic large-cell lymphoma[126–128]. In addition, immunostaining for LEMD1 has been reported in 35% (101/289) of OSCC specimens and closely involved in local progression (T factor), clinical stage, and nodal metastasis[129]. The disease-free survival among all LEMD1-positive patients was considerably worse compared to LEMD1-negative patients, and the LEMD1 expression was an independent prognosticator. In an in vitro analysis using OSCC cells, LEMD1 enhanced invasion ability. Moreover, we determined that LEMD1 controlled the intravasation and transmigration of OSCC cells to endothelial cells. Since CTA in cancer is a useful target of immunotherapy through the activation of CTL[130], LEMD1 normalization might be useful for activating the host immune function of OSCC. Perhaps, LEMD1 might be a novel tumor-promoting and prognostic CTA that induces the gain of invasion ability and transendothelial migration of OSCC.

2.11. PAUF

2.12. Pancreatic adenocarcinoma upregulated factor (PAUF) is a newly determined secretory protein in pancreatic cancer[131]. PAUF is a ligand for toll-like receptor 2 (TLR2) and TLR4 and can promote the migration, invasion, proliferation, angiogenesis, and CXC receptor type 4 (CXCR4)–mediated metastasis of pancreatic cancer cells[131–134]. In addition, PAUF contributes to the insufffiency of T-cell immunosurveillance and immunoescape through the migration and activation of myeloid-derived immature cells in pancreatic cancer[135]. Moreover, PAUF has been reported to decrease pancreatic cancer cells' sensitivity to gemcitabine and 5-FU[134]. Recently, we reportedthat PAUF facilitated growth, invasion, suppression of apoptosis, and cisplatin resistance in OSCC cells[136]. In an immunohistochemical analysis, PAUF expression was detected in 23.4% (52/222) of OSCC cases, and the immunoreactivity for PAUF markedly correlated with nodal metastasis. We also revealed that PAUF-positive patients exhibited a remarkably shorter disease-free and overall survival than PAUF-negative patients. Furthermore, a multivariate analysis revealed that PAUF expression was an independent prognostic predictor of poor disease-free survival and cancer-specifific mortality of OSCC patients. Thus, our findings indicate that PAUF is a useful molecular target for OSCC diagnosis and therapy.

2.13. ME1

Malic enzyme 1 (ME1) is a multifunctional protein involved in glycolysis, the citric acid cycle, NADPH production, glutamine metabolism, and lipogenesis[137]. In malignancies, ME1 overexpression correlated with unfavorable prognosis in HCC patients by EMT induction [137]. In addition, ME1 is associated with tumor growth, lung metastasis, peritoneal dissemination and shorter overall and disease-free survival in gastric cancer cases. Our experimental data suggested that ME1 promotes cancer progression by increasing lactate fermentation, maintaining redox status, acquiring stemness and EMT phenotype and promoting tumor growth and invasion in OSCC cells[74].

In addition, ME1 expression closely correlated with local progression (T factor), clinical stage, and nodal metastasis in human OSCC specimens. Furthermore, the survival analysis using the Kaplan–Meier method revealed that cases with moderate-to-strong ME1 expression exhibited markedly worse prognosis than those with weak ME1 expression. Since inhibiting ME1 suppressed tumor growth and increased survival time in a mouse tumor model, ME1 could be a valid target for molecular therapy in OSCC. Although advances in molecular oncological biology have elucidated OSCC molecular mechanisms, the prognosis of locoregionally and metastatically advanced cancer awaits improvement. Several studies about invasion, metastasis, and prognosis-related molecular biomarkers for malignancies, including OSCC, have been published to date. Recently, molecular-targeted therapy using cetuximab, an anti-EGFR-specific chimeric monoclonal antibody, and nivolumab, an antibody inhibitor of PD-1 receptor, is used in OSCC patients[138]. However, other targets for diagnosis and treatment of OSCC remain unknown, necessitating the development of useful molecular tumor markers. Hopefully, relevant novel tumor biomarkers will be established in the near future.

22. REFERENCES

1. Nardy, A.F.F.R., Freire-de-Lima, L., Freire-de-Lima, C.G., Morrot, A., 2016. The sweet side of immune evasion: role of glycans in the mechanisms of cancer progression. Front. Oncol. 6.

2. Pinho, S.S., Reis, C.A., 2015. Glycosylation in cancer: mechanisms and clinical implications. Nat. Rev. Canc. 15, 540.

3. Lemjabbar-Alaoui, H., Mckinney, A., Yang, Y.-W., Tran, V.M., Phillips, J.J., 2015. Chapter nine e glycosylation alterations in lung and brain cancer. In: Drake, R.R., Ball, L.E. (Eds.), Advances in Cancer Research. Academic Press.

4. Kim, J.W.; Park, Y.; Roh, J.L.; Cho, K.J.; Choi, S.H.; Nam, S.Y.; Kim, S.Y. Prognostic value of glucosylceramide synthase and P-glycoprotein expression in oral cavity cancer. *Int. J. Clin. Oncol.* **2016**, *21*, 883–889.

5. Gonzalez-Garcia, R.; Naval-Gias, L.; Rodriguez-Campo, F.J.; Sastre-Perez, J.; Munoz-Guerra, M.F.; Gil-Diez Usandizaga, J.L. Contralateral lymph neck node metastasis ofsquamous cell carcinoma of the oral cavity: a retrospective analytic study in 315 patients. *J. Oral Maxillofac. Surg.* **2008**, *66*, 1390–1398.

6. Ferreira JA, Magalhães A, Gomes J, Peixoto A, Gaiteiro C, Fernandes E, Santos LL, Reis CA. Protein glycosylation in gastric and colorectal cancers: Toward cancer detection and targeted therapeutics. Cancer Lett. 2017 Feb 28;387:32-45.

7. Sanderson, R.D., Yang, Y., Purushothaman, A., Khotskaya, Y.B., Ritchie, J.P., Ramani, V.C., 2010. Proteoglycans and cancer. In: Zent, R., Pozzi, A. (Eds.), Cellextracellular Matrix Interactions in Cancer. Springer New York, New York, NY.

8. Fernandez-Vega, I., Garcia-Suarez, O., Garcia, B., Crespo, A., Astudillo, A., Quiros, L.M., 2015. Heparan sulfate proteoglycans undergo differential expression alterations in right sided colorectal cancer, depending on their metastatic character. BMC Canc. 15, 742.

9. Ho, W.-L., Hsu, W.-M., Huang, M.-C., Kadomatsu, K., Nakagawara, A., 2016. Protein glycosylation in cancers and its potential therapeutic applications in neuroblastoma. J. Hematol. Oncol. 9, 100.

10. Dosaka-Akita, H., Kinoshita, I., Yamazaki, K., Izumi, H., Itoh, T., Katoh, H., Nishimura, M., Matsuo, K., Yamada, Y., Kohno, K., 2002. N-acetylgalactosaminyl transferase-3 is a potential new marker for non-small cell lung cancers. Br. J. Cancer 87, 751e755.

11. Park, J.H., Nishidate, T., Kijima, K., Ohashi, T., Takegawa, K., Fujikane, T., Hirata, K., Nakamura, Y., Katagiri, T., 2010. Critical roles of mucin 1 glycosylation by transactivated polypeptide N-acetylgalactosaminyltransferase 6 in mammary carcinogenesis. Cancer Res. 70, 2759e2769.

12. Itzkowitz, S.H., Yuan, M., Montgomery, C.K., Kjeldsen, T., Takahashi, H.K., Bigbee, W.L., Kim, Y.S., 1989. Expression of Tn, sialosyl-Tn, and T antigens in human colon cancer. Cancer Res. 49, 197e204.

13. Kaur, S., Kumar, S., Momi, N., Sasson, A.R., Batra, S.K., 2013. Mucins in pancreatic cancer and its microenvironment. Nat. Rev. Gastroenterol. Hepatol. 10, 607e620.

14. Hollingsworth, M.A., Swanson, B.J., 2004. Mucins in cancer: protection and control of the cell surface. Nat. Rev. Canc. 4, 45e60.

15. Chen, S.H., Dallas, M.R., Balzer, E.M., Konstantopoulos, K., 2012. Mucin 16 is a functional selectin ligand on pancreatic cancer cells. FASEB J. 26, 1349e1359.

16. Krause, T., Turner, G.A., 1999. Are selectins involved in metastasis? Clin. Exp. Metastasis 17, 183e192.

17. Burnet, M., 1957. Cancerda biological approach. I. The processes of control. II. The significance of somatic mutation. Br. Med. J. 1.

18. Pashov, A., Monzavi-Karbassi, B., Raghava, G.P., Kieber-Emmons, T., 2010. Bridging innate and adaptive antitumor immunity targeting glycans. J. Biomed. Biotechnol. 2010, 354068.

19. Li, C.W., Lim, S.O., Xia, W., Lee, H.H., Chan, L.C., Kuo, C.W., Khoo, K.H., Chang, S.S., Cha, J.H., Kim, T., Hsu, J.L., Wu, Y., Hsu, J.M., Yamaguchi, H., Ding, Q., Wang, Y., Yao, J., Lee, C.C., Wu, H.J., Sahin, A.A., Allison, J.P., Yu, D., Hortobagyi, G.N., Hung, M.C., 2016. Glycosylation and stabilization of programmed death ligand-1 suppresses T-cell activity. Nat. Commun. 7, 12632.

20. Kannagi, R., Izawa, M., Koike, T., Miyazaki, K., Kimura, N., 2004. Carbohydrate-mediated cell adhesion in cancer metastasis and angiogenesis. Cancer Sci. 95, 377e384.

21. Carrascal, M.A., Severino, P.F., Guadalupe Cabral, M., Silva, M., Ferreira, J.A., Calais, F., Quinto, H., Pen, C., Ligeiro, D., Santos, L.L., Dall'olio, F., Videira, P.A., 2014. Sialyl Tn-expressing bladder cancer cells induce a tolerogenic phenotype in innate and adaptive immune cells. Mol. Oncol. 8, 753e765.

22. Ohyama, C., Tsuboi, S., Fukuda, M., 1999. Dual roles of sialyl Lewis X oligosaccharides in tumor metastasis and rejection by natural killer cells. EMBO J. 18, 1516e1525.

23. Madsen, C.B., Petersen, C., Lavrsen, K., Harndahl, M., Buus, S., Clausen, H., Pedersen, A.E., Wandall, H.H., 2012. Cancer associated aberrant protein O-glycosylation can modify antigen processing and immune response. PLoS One 7, e50139.

24. Weissman IL (2000). Stem cells: units of development, units of regeneration, and units in evolution. Cell 100, 157–168.

25. Zhao W, Ji X, Zhang F, Li L, and Ma L (2012). Embryonic stem cell markers. Molecules 17, 6196–6236.

26. Yan Q, Yao D, Wei LL, Huang Y, Myers J, Zhang L, Xin W, Shim J, Man Y, and Petryniak B, et al (2010). O-fucose modulates Notch-controlled blood lineage commitment. Am J Pathol 176, 2921–2934.

27. Seth A, Machingo QJ, Fritz A, and Shur BD (2010). Core fucosylation is required for midline patterning during zebrafish development. Dev Dyn 239, 3380–3390.

28. Kannagi R, Cochran NA, Ishigami F, Hakomori S, Andrews PW, Knowles BB, and Solter D (1983). Stage-specific embryonic antigens (SSEA-3 and -4) are epitopes of a unique globo-series ganglioside isolated from human teratocarcinoma cells. EMBO J 2, 2355–2361.

29. Kannagi R, Levery SB, Ishigami F, Hakomori S, Shevinsky LH, Knowles BB, and Solter D (1983). New globoseries glycosphingolipids in human teratocarcinoma reactive with the monoclonal antibody directed to a developmentally regulated antigen, stage-specific embryonic antigen 3. J Biol Chem 258, 8934–8942.

30. Dulak J, Szade K, Szade A, Nowak W, and Jozkowicz A (2015). Adult stem cells: hopes and hypes of regenerative medicine. Acta Biochim Pol 62, 329–337.

31. Capela A and Temple S (2002). LeX/ssea-1 is expressed by adult mouse CNS stem cells, identifying them as nonependymal. Neuron 35, 865–875.

32. Yanagisawa M, Taga T, Nakamura K, Ariga T, and Yu RK (2005). Characterization of glycoconjugate antigens in mouse embryonic neural precursor cells. J Neurochem 95, 1311–1320.

33. Yagi H, Saito T, Yanagisawa M, Yu RK, and Kato K (2012). Lewis X-carrying N-glycans regulate the proliferation of mouse embryonic neural stem cells via the Notch signaling pathway. J Biol Chem 287, 24356–24364.

34. Yagi H and Kato K (2017). Functional roles of glycoconjugates in the maintenance of stemness and differentiation process of neural stem cells. Glycoconj J 34, 757–763.

35. Hamouda H, Ullah M, Berger M, Sittinger M, Tauber R, Ringe J, and Blanchard V (2013). N-glycosylation profile of undifferentiated and adipogenically differentiated human bone marrow mesenchymal stem cells: towards a next generation of stem cell markers. Stem Cells Dev 22, 3100–3113.

36. Sackstein R, Merzaban JS, Cain DW, Dagia NM, Spencer JA, Lin CP, and Wohlgemuth R (2008). Ex vivo glycan engineering of CD44 programs human multipotent mesenchymal stromal cell trafficking to bone. Nat Med 14, 181–187.

37. Miraglia S, Godfrey W, Yin AH, Atkins K, Warnke R, Holden JT, Bray RA, Waller EK, and Buck DW (1997). A novel five-transmembrane hematopoietic stem cell antigen: isolation, characterization, and molecular cloning. Blood 90, 5013–5021.

38. Zhou F, Cui C, Ge Y, Chen H, Li Q, Yang Z, Wu G, Sun S, Chen K, and Gu J, et al (2010). Alpha2,3-Sialylation regulates the stability of stem cell marker CD133. J Biochem 148, 273–280.

39. Vander Griend DJ, Karthaus WL, Dalrymple S, Meeker A, DeMarzo AM, and Isaacs JT (2008). The role of CD133 in normal human prostate stem cells and malignant cancer-initiating cells. Cancer Res 68, 9703–9711.

40. Zoller M (2015). CD44, hyaluronan, the hematopoietic stem cell, and leukemia-initiating cells. Front Immunol 6, 235.

41. He S, Nakada D, and Morrison SJ (2009). Mechanisms of stem cell selfrenewal. Annu Rev Cell Dev Biol 25, 377–406.

42. Sasaki N, Shinomi M, Hirano K, Ui-Tei K, and Nishihara S (2011). LacdiNAc (GalNAcbeta1-4GlcNAc) contributes to self-renewal of mouse embryonic stem cells by regulating leukemia inhibitory factor/STAT3 signaling. Stem Cells 29, 641–650.

43. Sasaki N, Okishio K, Ui-Tei K, Saigo K, Kinoshita-Toyoda A, Toyoda H, Nishimura T, Suda Y, Hayasaka M, and Hanaoka K, et al (2008). Heparan sulfate regulates self-renewal and pluripotency of embryonic stem cells. J Biol Chem 283, 3594–3606.

44. Kraushaar DC, Dalton S, and Wang L (2013). Heparan sulfate: a key regulator of embryonic stem cell fate. Biol Chem 394, 741–751.

45. Komekado H, Yamamoto H, Chiba T, and Kikuchi A (2007). Glycosylation and palmitoylation of Wnt-3a are coupled to produce an active form of Wnt-3a. Genes Cells 12, 521–534.

46. Duchesne L, Tissot B, Rudd TR, Dell A, and Fernig DG (2006). Nglycosylation of fibroblast growth factor receptor 1 regulates ligand and heparan sulfate co-receptor binding. J Biol Chem 281, 27178–27189.

47. Lee JM, Dedhar S, Kalluri R, and Thompson EW (2006). The epithelialmesenchymal transition: new insights in signaling, development, and disease. J Cell Biol 172, 973–981.

48. Thiery JP, Acloque H, Huang RY, and Nieto MA (2009). Epithelialmesenchymal transitions in development and disease. Cell 139, 871–890.

49. Hugo H, Ackland ML, Blick T, Lawrence MG, Clements JA, Williams ED, and Thompson EW (2007). Epithelial-mesenchymal and mesenchymal-epithelial transitions in carcinoma progression. J Cell Physiol 213, 374–383

50. Guan F, Handa K, and Hakomori SI (2009). Specific glycosphingolipids mediate epithelial-to-mesenchymal transition of human and mouse epithelial cell lines. Proc Natl Acad Sci U S A 106, 7461–7466.

51. Guan F, Schaffer L, Handa K, and Hakomori SI (2010). Functional role of gangliotetraosylceramide in epithelial-to-mesenchymal transition process induced by hypoxia and by TGF-{beta}. FASEB J 24, 4889–4903.

52. Freire-de-Lima L, Gelfenbeyn K, Ding Y, Mandel U, Clausen H, Handa K, and Hakomori SI (2011). Involvement of O-glycosylation defining oncofetal fibronectin in epithelial-mesenchymal transition process. Proc Natl Acad Sci U S A 108, 17690–17695.

53. Freire-de-Lima L (2014). Sweet and sour: the impact of differential glycosylation in cancer cells undergoing epithelial-mesenchymal transition. Front Oncol 4, 59.

54. Huanna T, Tao Z, Xiangfei W, Longfei A, Yuanyuan X, Jianhua W, Cuifang Z, Manjing J, Wenjing C, and Shaochuan Q, et al (2015). GALNT14 mediates tumor invasion and migration in breast cancer cell MCF-7. Mol Carcinog 54, 1159–1171.

55. Cheng S, Mao Q, Dong Y, Ren J, Su L, Liu J, Liu Q, Zhou J, Ye X, and Zheng S, et al (2017). GNB2L1 and its O-GlcNAcylation regulates metastasis via modulating epithelial-mesenchymal transition in the chemoresistance of gastric cancer. PLoS One 12e0182696.

56. Lucena MC, Carvalho-Cruz P, Donadio JL, Oliveira IA, de Queiroz RM, Marinho-Carvalho MM, Sola-Penna M, de Paula IF, Gondim KC, and McComb ME, et al (2016). Epithelial mesenchymal transition induces aberrant glycosylation through hexosamine biosynthetic pathway activation. J Biol Chem 291, 12917–12929.

57. Mallard BW and Tiralongo J (2017). Cancer stem cell marker glycosylation: nature, function and significance. Glycoconj J 34, 441–452.

58. Hakomori S (1996). Tumor malignancy defined by aberrant glycosylation and sphingo (glyco)lipid metabolism. Cancer Res 56, 5309–5318.

59. Yan Y, Zuo X, and Wei D (2015). Concise review: emerging role of CD44 in cancer stem cells: a promising biomarker and therapeutic target. Stem Cells Transl Med 4, 1033–1043.

60. Camp RL, Kraus TA, and Pure E (1991). Variations in the cytoskeletal interaction and posttranslational modification of the CD44 homing receptor in macrophages. J Cell Biol 115, 1283–1292.

61. Underhill C (1992). CD44: the hyaluronan receptor. J Cell Sci 103(Pt 2), 293–298.

62. Bartolazzi A, Nocks A, Aruffo A, Spring F, and Stamenkovic I (1996). of CD44 is implicated in CD44-mediated cell adhesion to hyaluronan. J Cell Biol 132, 1199–1208.

63. Catterall JB, Jones LM, and Turner GA (1999). Membrane protein glycosylation and CD44 content in the adhesion of human ovarian cancer cells to hyaluronan. Clin Exp Metastasis 17, 583–591.

64. Skelton TP, Zeng C, Nocks A, and Stamenkovic I (1998). Glycosylation provides both stimulatory and inhibitory effects on cell surface and soluble CD44 binding to hyaluronan. J Cell Biol 140, 431–446.

65. Rodgers AK, Nair A, Binkley PA, Tekmal R, and Schenken RS (2011). Inhibition of CD44 N- and O-linked glycosylation decreases endometrial cell lines attachment to peritoneal mesothelial cells. Fertil Steril 95, 823–825.

66. Goupille C, Hallouin F, Meflah K, and Le Pendu J (1997). Increase of rat colon carcinoma cells tumorigenicity by alpha(1-2) fucosyltransferase gene transfection. Glycobiology 7, 221–229.

67. Hallouin F, Goupille C, Bureau V, Meflah K, and Le Pendu J (1999). Increased tumorigenicity of rat colon carcinoma cells after alpha1,2-fucosyltransferase FTA anti-sense cDNA transfection. Int J Cancer 80, 606–611.

68. Singh R, Campbell BJ, Yu LG, Fernig DG, Milton JD, Goodlad RA, FitzGerald AJ, and Rhodes JM (2001). Cell surface-expressed ThomsenFriedenreich antigen in colon cancer is predominantly carried on high molecular weight splice variants of CD44. Glycobiology 11, 587–592.

69. Lin WM, Karsten U, Goletz S, Cheng RC, and Cao Y (2011). Expression of CD176 (Thomsen-Friedenreich antigen) on lung, breast and liver cancerinitiating cells. Int J Exp Pathol 92, 97–105.

70. Lin WM, Karsten U, Goletz S, Cheng RC, and Cao Y (2010). Co-expression of CD173 (H2) and CD174 (Lewis Y) with CD44 suggests that fucosylated histo blood group antigens are markers of breast cancer-initiating cells. Virchows Arch 456, 403–409.

71. Katoh Y and Katoh M (2007). Comparative genomics on PROM1 gene encoding stem cell marker CD133. Int J Mol Med 19, 967–970.

72. Bidlingmaier S, Zhu X, and Liu B (2008). The utility and limitations of glycosylated human CD133 epitopes in defining cancer stem cells. J Mol Med 86, 1025–1032.

73. Kemper K, Sprick MR, de Bree M, Scopelliti A, Vermeulen L, Hoek M, Zeilstra J, Pals ST, Mehmet H, and Stassi G, et al (2010). The AC133 epitope, but not the CD133 protein, is lost upon cancer stem cell differentiation.Cancer Res 70, 719–729.

74. Osmond TL, Broadley KW, and McConnell MJ (2010). Glioblastoma cells negative for the anti-CD133 antibody AC133 express a truncated variant of the CD133 protein. Int J Mol Med 25, 883–888.

75. Hemmoranta H, Satomaa T, Blomqvist M, Heiskanen A, Aitio O, Saarinen J, Natunen J, Partanen J, Laine J, and Jaatinen T (2007). N-glycan structures and associated gene expression reflect the characteristic N-glycosylation pattern of human hematopoietic stem and progenitor cells. Exp Hematol 35, 1279–1292.

76. Iida H, Suzuki M, Goitsuka R, and Ueno H (2012). Hypoxia induces CD133 expression in human lung cancer cells by up-regulation of OCT3/4 and SOX2. Int J Oncol 40, 71–79.

77. Lehnus KS, Donovan LK, Huang X, Zhao N, Warr TJ, Pilkington GJ, and An Q (2013). CD133 glycosylation is enhanced by hypoxia in cultured glioma stem cells. Int J Oncol 42, 1011–1017.

78. Liu Y, Ren S, Xie L, Cui C, Xing Y, Liu C, Cao B, Yang F, Li Y, and Chen X, et al (2015). Mutation of N-linked glycosylation at Asn548 in CD133 decreases its ability to promote hepatoma cell growth. Oncotarget 6, 20650–20660.

79. Springer T, Galfre G, Secher DS, and Milstein C (1978). Monoclonal xenogeneic antibodies to murine cell surface antigens: identification of novel leukocyte differentiation antigens. Eur J Immunol 8, 539–551.

80. Fang X, Zheng P, Tang J, and Liu Y (2010). CD24: from A to Z. Cell Mol Immunol 7, 100–103.

81. Kay R, Rosten PM, and Humphries RK (1991). CD24, a signal transducer modulating B cell activation responses, is a very short

peptide with a glycosyl phosphatidylinositol membrane anchor. J Immunol 147, 1412–1416.

82. Kristiansen G, Sammar M, and Altevogt P (2004). Tumour biological aspects of CD24, a mucin-like adhesion molecule. J Mol Histol 35, 255–262.

83. Kristiansen G, Winzer KJ, Mayordomo E, Bellach J, Schluns K, Denkert C, Dahl E, Pilarsky C, Altevogt P, and Guski H, et al (2003). CD24 expression is a new prognostic marker in breast cancer. Clin Cancer Res 9, 4906–4913.

84. Zheng J, Li Y, Yang J, Liu Q, Shi M, Zhang R, Shi H, Ren Q, Ma J, and Guo H, et al (2011). NDRG2 inhibits hepatocellular carcinoma adhesion, migration and invasion by regulating CD24 expression. BMC Cancer 11(251), 251–259.

85. Lee HJ, Choe G, Jheon S, Sung SW, Lee CT, and Chung JH (2010). CD24, a novel cancer biomarker, predicting disease-free survival of non-small cell lung carcinomas: a retrospective study of prognostic factor analysis from the viewpoint of forthcoming (seventh) new TNM classification. J Thorac Oncol 5, 649–657.

86. Visvader JE and Lindeman GJ (2008). Cancer stem cells in solid tumours: accumulating evidence and unresolved questions. Nat Rev Cancer 8, 755–768.

87. Aigner S, Ramos CL, Hafezi-Moghadam A, Lawrence MB, Friederichs J, Altevogt P, and Ley K (1998). CD24 mediates rolling of breast carcinoma cells on P-selectin. FASEB J 12, 1241–1251.

88. Yeung TM, Gandhi SC, Wilding JL, Muschel R, and Bodmer WF (2010). Cancer stem cells from colorectal cancer-derived cell lines. Proc Natl Acad Sci U S A 107, 3722–3727.

89. Wei X, Dombkowski D, Meirelles K, Pieretti-Vanmarcke R, Szotek PP, Chang HL, Preffer FI, Mueller PR, Teixeira J, and MacLaughlin DT, et al (2010). Mullerian inhibiting substance preferentially inhibits stem/progenitors in human ovarian cancer cell lines compared with chemotherapeutics. Proc Natl Acad Sci U S A 107, 18874–18879.

90. Gao MQ, Han YT, Zhu L, Chen SG, Hong ZY, andWang CB (2009). Cytotoxicity of natural extract from Tegillarca granosa on ovarian cancer cells is mediated by multiple molecules. Clin Invest Med 32, E368-375.

91. Gao MQ, Choi YP, Kang S, Youn JH, and Cho NH (2010). CD24+ cells from hierarchically organized ovarian cancer are enriched in cancer stem cells. Oncogene 29, 2672–2680.

92. Su D, Deng H, Zhao X, Zhang X, Chen L, Chen X, Li Z, Bai Y, Wang Y, and Zhong Q, et al (2009). Targeting CD24 for treatment of ovarian cancer by short hairpin RNA. Cytotherapy 11, 642–652.

93. Yang CH, Wang HL, Lin YS, Kumar KP, Lin HC, Chang CJ, Lu CC, Huang TT, Martel J, and Ojcius DM, et al (2014). Identification of CD24 as a cancer stem cell marker in human nasopharyngeal carcinoma. PLoS One 9e99412.

94. Lee CJ, Dosch J, and Simeone DM (2008). Pancreatic cancer stem cells. J Clin Oncol 26, 2806–2812.

95.   Ricardo S, Vieira AF, Gerhard R, Leitao D, Pinto R, Cameselle-Teijeiro JF, Milanezi F, Schmitt F, and Paredes J (2011). Breast cancer stem cell markers CD44, CD24 and ALDH1: expression distribution within intrinsic molecular subtype. J Clin Pathol 64, 937–946.

96.   Hurt EM, Kawasaki BT, Klarmann GJ, Thomas SB, and Farrar WL (2008). CD44+ CD24(-) prostate cells are early cancer progenitor/stem cells that provide a model for patients with poor prognosis. Br J Cancer 98, 756–765.

97.   Friederichs J, Zeller Y, Hafezi-Moghadam A, Grone HJ, Ley K, and Altevogt P (2000). The CD24/P-selectin binding pathway initiates lung arrest of human A125 adenocarcinoma cells. Cancer Res 60, 6714–6722.

98.   Overdevest JB, Thomas S, Kristiansen G, Hansel DE, Smith SC, and Theodorescu D (2011). CD24 offers a therapeutic target for control of bladder cancer metastasis based on a requirement for lung colonization. Cancer Res 71, 3802–3811.

99.   Baeuerle PA and Gires O (2007). EpCAM (CD326) finding its role in cancer. Br J Cancer 96, 417–423.

100.   Munz M, Kieu C, Mack B, Schmitt B, Zeidler R, and Gires O (2004). The carcinoma-associated antigen EpCAM upregulates c-myc and induces cell proliferation. Oncogene 23, 5748–5758.

101.   Munz M, Zeidler R, and Gires O (2005). The tumour-associated antigen EpCAM upregulates the fatty acid binding protein E-FABP. Cancer Lett 225, 151–157.

102. Lu TY, Lu RM, Liao MY, Yu J, Chung CH, Kao CF, and Wu HC (2010). Epithelial cell adhesion molecule regulation is associated with the maintenance of the undifferentiated phenotype of human embryonic stem cells. J Biol Chem 285, 8719–8732.

103. Ng VY, Ang SN, Chan JX, and Choo AB (2010). Characterization of epithelial cell adhesion molecule as a surface marker on undifferentiated human embryonic stem cells. Stem Cells 28, 29–35.

104. Chong JM and Speicher DW (2001). Determination of disulfide bond assignments and N-glycosylation sites of the human gastrointestinal carcinoma antigen GA733-2 (CO17-1A, EGP, KS1-4, KSA, and Ep-CAM). J Biol Chem 276, 5804–5813.

105. Pauli C, Münz M, Kieu C, Mack B, Breinl P, Wollenberg B, Lang S, Zeidler R, and Gires O (2003). Tumor-specific glycosylation of the carcinoma-associated epithelial cell adhesion molecule EpCAM in head and neck carcinomas. Cancer Lett 193, 25–32.

106. Munz M, Fellinger K, Hofmann T, Schmitt B, and Gires O (2008). Glycosylation is crucial for stability of tumour and cancer stem cell antigen EpCAM. Front Biosci (13), 5195–5201.

107. Zhang D, Liu X, Gao J, Sun Y, Liu T, Yan Q, and Yang X (2017). The role of epithelial cell adhesion molecule N-glycosylation on apoptosis in breast cancer cells. Tumour Biol 39, 1–8.

108. Corfield AP (2015). Mucins: a biologically relevant glycan barrier in mucosal protection. Biochim Biophys Acta 1850, 236–252.

109. Joshi S, Kumar S, Choudhury A, Ponnusamy MP, and Batra SK (2014). Altered Mucins (MUC) trafficking in benign and malignant conditions. Oncotarget 5, 7272–7284.

110. Das S and Batra SK (2015). Understanding the unique attributes of MUC16 (CA125): potential implications in targeted therapy. Cancer Res 75, 4669–4674.

111. Lakshmanan I, Ponnusamy MP, Macha MA, Haridas D, Majhi PD, Kaur S, Jain M, Batra SK, and Ganti AK (2015). Mucins in lung cancer: diagnostic, prognostic, and therapeutic implications. J Thorac Oncol 10, 19–27.

112. Hanson RL and Hollingsworth MA (2016). Functional consequences of differential O-glycosylation of MUC1, MUC4, and MUC16 (downstream effects on signaling). Biomolecules 6, E34.

113. Krishn SR, Kaur S, Smith LM, Johansson SL, Jain M, Patel A, Gautam SK, Hollingsworth MA, Mandel U, and Clausen H, et al (2016). Mucins and associated glycan signatures in colon adenoma-carcinoma sequence: prospective pathological implication(s) for early diagnosis of colon cancer. Cancer Lett 374, 304–314.

114. Kaur S, Kumar S, Momi N, Sasson AR, and Batra SK (2013). Mucins in pancreatic cancer and its microenvironment. Nat Rev Gastroenterol Hepatol 10, 607–620.

115. Nath S and Mukherjee P (2014). MUC1: a multifaceted oncoprotein with a key role in cancer progression. Trends Mol Med 20, 332–342.

116. Hikita ST, Kosik KS, Clegg DO, and Bamdad C (2008). MUC1* mediates the growth of human pluripotent stem cells. PLoS One 3e3312.

117. Curry JM, Thompson KJ, Rao SG, Besmer DM, Murphy AM, Grdzelishvili VZ, Ahrens WA, McKillop IH, Sindram D, and Iannitti DA, et al (2013). The use of a novel MUC1 antibody to identify cancer stem cells and circulating MUC1 in mice and patients with pancreatic cancer. J Surg Oncol 107, 713–722.

118. Fatrai S, Schepers H, Tadema H, Vellenga E, Daenen SM, and Schuringa JJ (2008). Mucin1 expression is enriched in the human stem cell fraction of cord blood and is upregulated in majority of the AML cases. Exp Hematol 36, 1254–1265.

119. Stroopinsky D, Rosenblatt J, Ito K, Mills H, Yin L, Rajabi H, Vasir B, Kufe T, Luptakova K, and Arnason J, et al (2013). MUC1 is a potential target for the treatment of acute myeloid leukemia stem cells. Cancer Res 73, 5569–5579.

120. Engelmann K, Shen H, and Finn OJ (2008). MCF7 side population cells with characteristics of cancer stem/progenitor cells express the tumor antigen MUC1. Cancer Res 68, 2419–2426.

121. Zhou N, Zhang Y, Zhang X, Lei Z, Hu R, Li H, Mao Y, Wang X, Irwin DM, and Niu G, et al (2015). Exposure of tumor-associated macrophages to apoptotic MCF-7 cells promotes breast cancer growth and metastasis. Int J Mol Sci 16, 11966–11982.

122. Zhou N, Wang R, Zhang Y, Lei Z, Zhang X, Hu R, Li H, Mao Y, Wang X, and Irwin DM, et al (2015). Staurosporine induced apoptosis may activate cancer stem-like cells (CD44(+)/CD24(−)) in MCF-7 by upregulating Mucin1 and EpCAM. J Cancer 6, 1049–1057.

123. Gautam SK, Kumar S, Cannon A, Hall B, Bhatia R, Nasser MW, Mahapatra S, Batra SK, and Jain M (2017). MUC4 mucin—a

therapeutic target for pancreatic ductal adenocarcinoma. Expert Opin Ther Targets 21, 657–669.

124. Ponnusamy MP, Seshacharyulu P, Vaz A, Dey P, and Batra SK (2011). MUC4 stabilizes HER2 expression and maintains the cancer stem cell population in ovarian cancer cells. J Ovarian Res 4, 7.

125. Mimeault M, Johansson SL, Senapati S, Momi N, Chakraborty S, and Batra SK (2010). MUC4 down-regulation reverses chemoresistance of pancreatic cancer stem/progenitor cells and their progenies. Cancer Lett 295, 69–84.

126. Zhang H, Yang Y, Wang Y, Gao X, Wang W, Liu H, He H, Liang Y, Pan K, and Wu H, et al (2015). Relationship of tumor marker CA125 and ovarian tumor stem cells: preliminary identification. J Ovarian Res 8, 19.

127. Das S, Rachagani S, Torres-Gonzalez MP, Lakshmanan I, Majhi PD, Smith LM, Wagner KU, and Batra SK (2015). Carboxyl-terminal domain of MUC16 imparts tumorigenic and metastatic functions through nuclear translocation of JAK2 to pancreatic cancer cells. Oncotarget 6, 5772–5787.

128. Liu YY, Hill RA, and Li YT (2013). Ceramide glycosylation catalyzed by glucosylceramide synthase and cancer drug resistance. Adv Cancer Res 117, 59–89.

129. Gupta V, Bhinge KN, Hosain SB, Xiong K, Gu X, Shi R, Ho MY, Khoo KH, Li SC, and Li YT, et al (2012). Ceramide glycosylation by glucosylceramide synthase selectively maintains the properties of breast cancer stem cells. J Biol Chem 287, 37195–37205.

130. Liu YY, Patwardhan GA, Bhinge K, Gupta V, Gu X, and Jazwinski SM (2011). Suppression of glucosylceramide synthase restores p53-dependent apoptosis in mutant p53 cancer cells. Cancer Res 71, 2276–2285.

131. Patwardhan GA, Hosain SB, Liu DX, Khiste SK, Zhao Y, Bielawski J, Jazwinski SM, and Liu YY (2014). Ceramide modulates pre-mRNA splicing to restore the expression of wild-type tumor suppressor p53 in deletion-mutant cancer cells. Biochim Biophys Acta 1841, 1571–1580.

132. Hosain SB, Khiste SK, Uddin MB, Vorubindi V, Ingram C, Zhang S, Hill RA, Gu X, and Liu YY (2016). Inhibition of glucosylceramide synthase eliminates the oncogenic function of p53 R273H mutant in the epithelial-mesenchymal transition and induced pluripotency of colon cancer cells.Oncotarget 7, 60575–60592.

133. Che MI, Huang J, Hung JS, Lin YC, Huang MJ, Lai HS, Hsu WM, Liang JT, and Huang MC (2014). beta1, 4-N-acetylgalactosaminyl transferase III modulates cancer stemness through EGFR signaling pathway in colon cancer cells. Oncotarget 5, 3673–/3684.

134. Guo H, Nagy T, and Pierce M (2014). Post-translational glycoprotein modifications regulate colon cancer stem cells and colon adenoma progression in Apc(min/+) mice through altered Wnt receptor signaling. J Biol Chem 289, 31534–31549.

135. Terao N, Takamatsu S, Minehira T, Sobajima T, Nakayama K, Kamada Y, and Miyoshi E (2015). Fucosylation is a common glycosylation type in pancreatic cancer stem cell-like phenotypes. World J Gastroenterol 3876–3887.

136. Schultz MJ, Holdbrooks AT, Chakraborty A, Grizzle WE, Landen CN, Buchsbaum DJ, Conner MG, Arend RC, Yoon KJ, and Klug CA, et al (2016). The tumor-associated glycosyltransferase ST6Gal-I regulates stem cell transcription factors and confers a cancer stem cell phenotype. Cancer Res 76, 3978–3988.

137. Li C, Du Y, Yang Z, He L, Wang Y, Hao L, Ding M, Yan R, Wang J, and Fan Z (2016). GALNT1-mediated glycosylation and activation of sonic hedgehog signaling maintains the self-renewal and tumor-initiating capacity of bladder cancer stem cells. Cancer Res 76, 1273–1283.